T0042046

EXPLORE!

☞ THE MOST DANGEROUS JOURNEYS OF ALL TIME

DEBORAH KESPERT

EXPLORE!

THE MOST DANGEROUS JOURNEYS OF ALL TIME

CONTENTS

LA FLORIDA

GREAT EXPLORERS

Centuries ago, daring adventurers crossed lands and oceans to piece together the shape of our planet. Today, people have explored most of the Earth's surface, so instead they attempt new challenges: traveling to the ocean depths or into space. Perhaps the great explorers in this timeline will inspire you to climb a mountain, dive to the bottom of the sea or even fly to another planet!

KEY TO TIMELINE

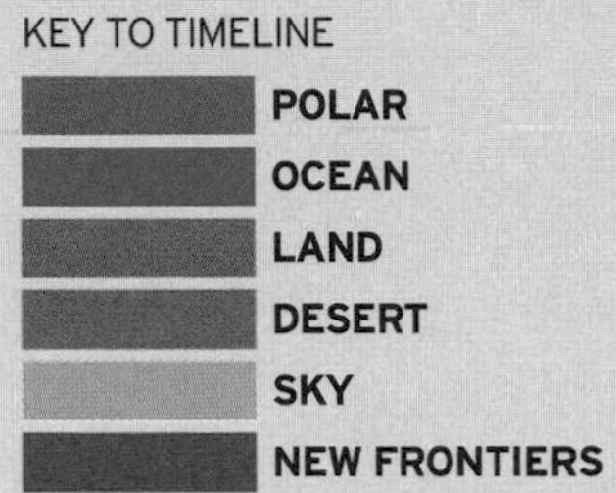

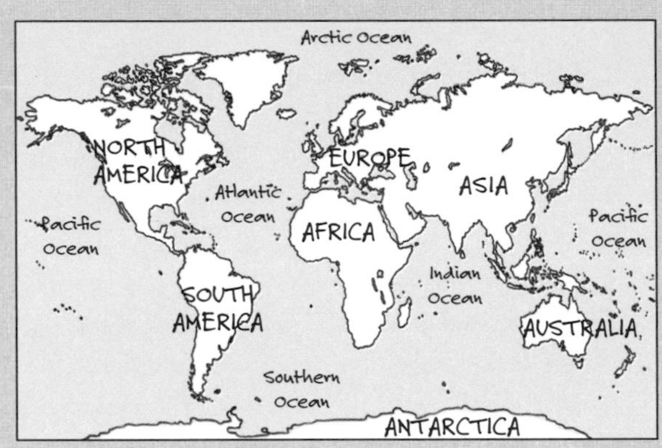

→ On this world map, you can see the continents and oceans. Match this map to the world maps inside the book.

1200s →	1271–95	**Marco Polo** travels to China.
1300s →	1325	**Ibn Battuta** explores Asia and Africa for 30 years.
1400s →	1434	**Gil Eanes** sails around the coast of West Africa.
	1492–93	**Christopher Columbus** discovers the Americas.
	1497–99	**Vasco da Gama** becomes the first European to travel by sea to India.
1500s →	1519	**Hernán Cortés** arrives on the coast of Mexico and claims land for the Spanish.
	1519–22	**Ferdinand Magellan** is first to sail across the Pacific Ocean.
	1539–43	**Hernando de Soto** travels through Florida in North America.
	1577–80	**Francis Drake** sails around the world.
1600s →	1606	**Willem Janszoon** becomes the first known European to reach Australia.
	1642–43	**Abel Tasman** discovers Tasmania and sails along the coast of New Zealand.
	1648	**Semyon Dezhnyov** discovers a sea passage between Russia and Alaska.
1700s →	1741	**Vitus Bering** discovers Alaska for Russia.
	1761–63	**Carsten Niebuhr and Peter Forsskål** travel through Arabia collecting specimens.
	1768–71	**James Cook** sails from England to Australia.
	1783	**The Montgolfier brothers** launch the first passengers in a hot air balloon.
1800s →	1804–06	**Meriwether Lewis and William Clark** lead the first expedition west across the United States.
	1828	**René Caillié** is the first European to travel to Timbuktu in Africa.
	1839	**Edward John Eyre** leads expeditions to the deserts of southern Australia.
	1839–43	**James Clark Ross** sails around the coast of Antarctica.
	1850–54	**Robert McClure** travels up the Northwest Passage in the Arctic.
	1853–56	**David Livingstone** is the first European to cross Africa.
	1853	**Richard Burton** treks across Arabia.
	1860–61	**Robert O'Hara Burke and William John Wills** make the first crossing of Australia.
	1894–95	**Mary Kingsley** travels solo to West Africa.

Polar
Roald Amundsen

Ocean
Christopher Columbus

Land
Marco Polo

Desert
Wilfred Thesiger

Sky
Amelia Earhart

New Frontiers
Yuri Gagarin

1900s →	1900	**Aurel Stein** begins a series of journeys to Central Asia.
	1903	**The Wright brothers** make the first successful powered flight.
	1909	**Robert Peary** claims to be the first to have reached the North Pole.
	1909	**Louis Blériot** makes the first flight across the English Channel.
	1911	**Robert Scott and Roald Amundsen** race to be first to the South Pole.
	1911–12	**Nobu Shirase** leads the first Japanese attempt to reach the South Pole.
	1913–14	**Gertrude Bell** is one of the first European women to explore the Arabian Desert.
	1914	**T. E. Lawrence** makes a military survey of the Negev Desert.
	1914	**Ernest Shackleton** leads an ill-fated expedition to cross Antarctica.
	1919	**John Alcock and Arthur Whitten Brown** make the first non-stop flight across the Atlantic Ocean.
	1927	**Freya Stark** begins a series of travels in the Middle East.
	1927	**Charles Lindbergh** flies solo non-stop across the Atlantic Ocean.
	1928	**Kingsford Smith and Charles Ulm** make the first flight across the Pacific Ocean.
	1929	**Richard Byrd** makes the first flight over the South Pole.
	1932	**Amelia Earhart** is the first woman to fly solo across the Atlantic Ocean.
	1946–47	**Wilfred Thesiger** treks across deserts on the Arabian Peninsula.
	1951–55	**Jacques-Yves Cousteau** explores the Mediterranean Sea, Red Sea and Indian Ocean.
	1953	**Edmund Hillary and Tenzing Norgay** are the first to the top of Mount Everest.
	1960	**Jacques Piccard and Don Walsh** explore the deepest part of the Atlantic Ocean.
	1961	**Yuri Gagarin** becomes the first person to travel into space and orbits the Earth.
	1963	**Valentina Tereshkova** is the first woman in space.
	1969	**Wally Herbert** is the first man to walk undisputed to the North Pole.
	1969	**Neil Armstrong** becomes the first person to stand on the Moon.
	1980	**Reinhold Messner** is the first to climb Mount Everest solo without extra oxygen.
	1989	**Robert Swan** is the first person to walk to both Poles.
	1979–82	**Ranulph Fiennes** makes the first transglobe expedition.
	1985	**Richard Bass** is first to climb the highest summits on all seven continents.
	1993	**Ranulph Fiennes** crosses the Antarctic continent on foot.
	1994	**Erling Kagge** is first to reach the North Pole, South Pole and the summit of Mount Everest.
	1999	**Bertrand Piccard and Brian Jones** make the first non-stop balloon flight around the world.
2000s →	2001	**Dennis Tito** is the world's first space tourist – paying for a trip into space.
	2003	**Sibusiso Vilane** is the first black African to reach the top of Mount Everest.
	2010	**Ed Stafford** is first to walk the length of the Amazon River.
	2011	**Amelia Hempleman-Adams,** aged 16, becomes one of the youngest to ski to the South Pole.
	2012	**James Cameron** dives solo to the deepest point in the ocean in a submersible.
	2012	**Felix Baumgartner** skydives from the edge of space faster than the speed of sound.

RACE TO THE SOUTH POLE

THE CHALLENGE

 A brutal race across the coldest continent on Earth to become the first person to reach the South Pole.

DANGERS

Ferocious winds; all supplies carried; no contact with the world; sub-zero temperatures

WHO **ROBERT SCOTT** and **ROALD AMUNDSEN**
WHERE Antarctica, where temperatures can reach -89.2ºC
WHEN October 1911 to December 1911
HOW by foot, ski, ponies and dog sled
DISTANCE about 3,000 km (1,860 miles)
WHY to reach the southernmost point on the Earth's surface

BACKGROUND

For centuries explorers had scoured the Southern Ocean, hunting for shipping routes or whales. Then, in 1911, international rivals set out to be the first to reach the South Pole.

→ Explorers stand in a grotto in an iceberg while Scott's ship *Terra Nova*, meaning "new land," sits in ice.

RACE TO THE

SOUTH POLE

☞ Who would win the prize of reaching the South Pole first?

In 1902, Captain Robert Falcon Scott got to within 770 km (480 miles) of the South Pole and returned home a hero. Scott was bitten by "Pole-mania" and he began organizing special motor-powered sleds to help him make it to the Pole on his next trip. But, as he prepared, another celebrated explorer called Roald Amundsen was secretly planning an expedition of his own.

Amundsen had wanted to be first to reach the North Pole. After he heard that a US expedition had beaten him to it, he decided instead to head south. The Norwegian was sure that his team's skis and dogs would work just as well in the Antarctic. By early 1911, both Scott and Amundsen had landed their boats and were unpacking the supplies they would need to reach the South Pole. They would be living in freezing conditions on the ice for nearly a year.

ANTARCTICA
South Pole
Axel Heiberg Glacier
Beardmore Glacier
Transantarctic Mountains
Ross Sea Ice Shelf
Framheim
final camp
storage camp
Cape Evans
Scott's route
Amundsen's route

↑ This map shows the routes the teams took from the edge of Antarctica to the South Pole. Amundsen's journey was shorter than Scott's because he traveled over the Axel Heiberg Glacier – an expanse of ice that cuts through the deadly Transantarctic Mountains.

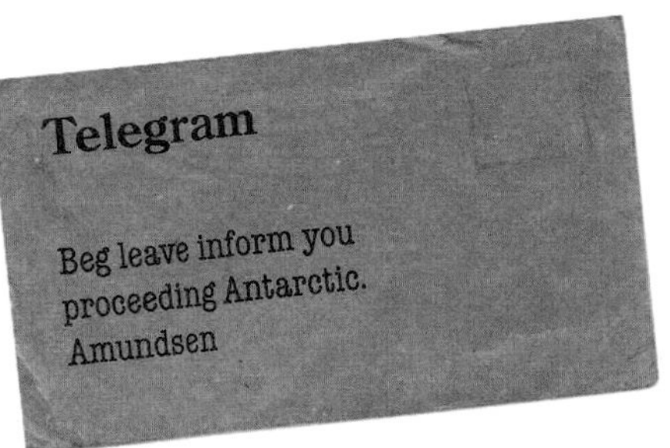

Telegram

Beg leave inform you proceeding Antarctic. Amundsen

↑ At first Amundsen tried to keep the destination of his expedition a secret. Then later, when Scott was already on his way, Amundsen sent a telegram to say that he was heading for the South Pole too.

↑ Scott's crew look out over a creaking ice floe. The ship had to be reinforced with 2 m (over 6 ft) of oak timber to protect her from the crushing ice.

DANGER!

WATCH OUT

Antarctica is ...

- >> the coldest place on Earth
- >> the windiest place on Earth
- >> one of Earth's driest places
- >> 99% covered with ice

↑Scott's crew before they reached the South Pole.

It would have been impossible for either expedition to go straight to the Pole without stopping – the food and fuel they needed was too much to be carried in one go. Instead, the teams had to create "storage camps," each a little closer to the Pole, to be used as stepping stones on their final trip. When the stores were ready, both parties settled down to wait until the weather was warmer, and the race could begin!

Amundsen set off, with Scott following less than two weeks later. Skilled at skiing and handling dogs, Amundsen's team was much quicker across the ice. Scott's men had a harder time – hauling their sleds for much of the distance meant they needed more food and had less time to rest.

HOW TO ...

Avoid Frostbite

Frostbite happens when parts of the body, especially the nose, fingers, toes and ears, freeze. In the worst cases, skin can blister and turn black! Here are some tips to prevent it.

1. Wear layers of clothing such as thick mittens and woolly socks.
2. A face mask or scarf will protect the nose and ears.
3. Keep your muscles moving – wiggle your fingers and toes, and smile and frown.

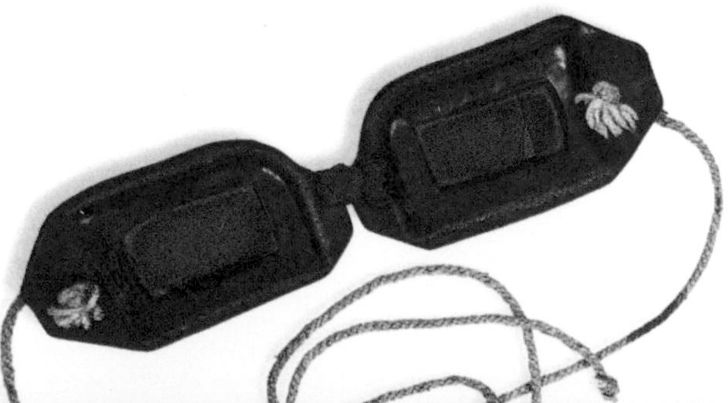

←The low sun at the South Pole reflects off the white snow, which can harm the eyes and make it difficult to see. Colored goggles such as these helped.

Who would win the prize of reaching the South Pole first?

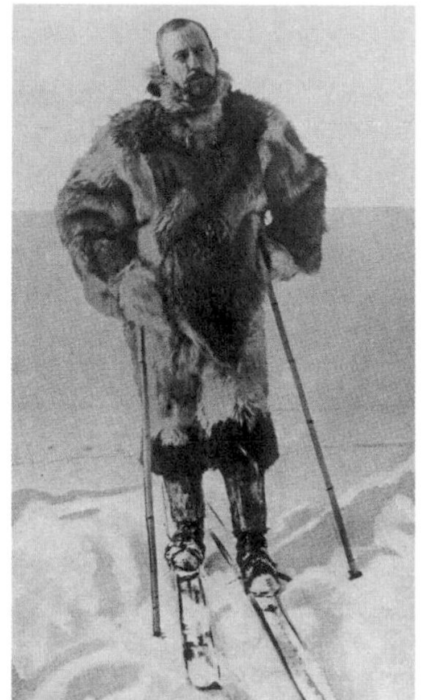

To keep warm and dry, Amundsen (above) and his crew dressed in the skins of reindeer and seals. Scott's team wore cotton clothing. As they worked up a sweat, the cotton froze.

Scott's supplies included tins of syrup, chocolate and boxes of sugar. In the freezing cold, the team relied on energy-giving foods such as these to provide the strength to carry on.

When Amundsen reached the Pole in December 1911, Scott and his men still had 580 km (360 miles) to go. The team pushed on across a high flat plain of ice in the bitter cold, making slow but steady progress. The men also stopped along the way to take surveys and carry out scientific investigations in this strange new landscape.

After a grueling journey lasting nearly three months, they finally approached the Pole. To their dismay, they spotted tracks in the snow and, in the distance, a Norwegian flag. Amundsen's team had beaten them. Exhausted, Scott wrote in his diary: "The worst has happened ... All the daydreams must go ... This is an awful place."

Scott's crew included a large group of scientists but for the final part of the journey he took only four other men with him.

POLAR RACE
This timeline traces the race to the South Pole and back. It starts with the departure of both teams from their base camps at the edge of the Antarctic ice.

1911 19 October — Amundsen and his crew set off.

1 November — Scott's team leaves 13 days later.

14 December — Amundsen reaches the South Pole first. It takes him just eight weeks.

1912 17 January — With 12 km (7 miles) to go, Scott discovers Amundsen has beaten him.

↑ Scott and his men stand next to Amundsen's tent at the South Pole.

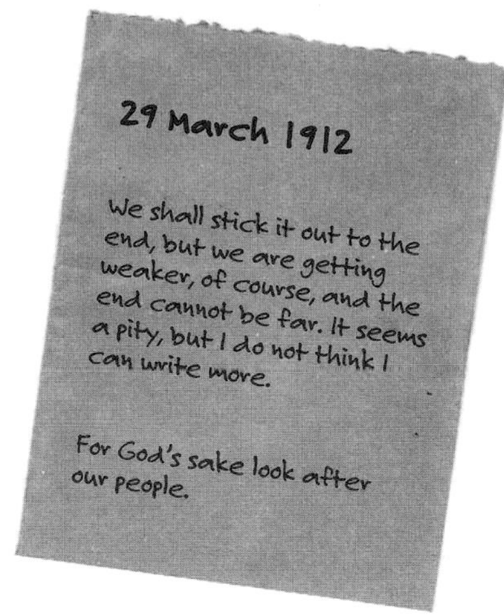

29 March 1912

We shall stick it out to the end, but we are getting weaker, of course, and the end cannot be far. It seems a pity, but I do not think I can write more.

For God's sake look after our people.

↑ Much of the information we have about Scott's expedition comes from his diaries. These are the last words he ever wrote.

The journey back was swift for Amundsen but not for Scott. Blizzards, extreme even for the Antarctic, were raging, supplies were short and the men were weak. In Scott's team, Evans was injured in a fall and died from the cold. Oates suffered severe frostbite and walked off to die alone because he didn't want to slow the others down. The remaining members lost their lives after eight days inside a tent with no water or food, just 18 km (11 miles) from a store of supplies.

Although Amundsen won the race to the South Pole and his skills as a polar explorer were truly impressive, Scott and his men have taught us much more about Antarctica. On their journey, they collected vast amounts of scientific data that helped us to shape our view of this icy continent today. Scott's team are also remembered for their incredible courage, determination and bravery in the face of the worst conditions you could ever imagine.

↑ This deepwater fish, named after Scott, is just one of many specimens collected by his scientists at the start of the Antarctic expedition.

18 January	**19 January**	**25 January**	**16 March**	**29 March**	**12 November**
Weary, Scott and his men make it to the South Pole.	Scott's crew begins the long and difficult journey home.	Amundsen arrives back at base. His expedition has taken just over three months.	Captain Oates walks to his death. Captain Evans has already died a month earlier.	Scott makes his last diary entry.	A search party finds Scott's tent, his diaries and the remaining bodies.

VOYAGE TO NEW WORLDS

THE CHALLENGE	 A sea expedition around the world, sailing west rather than east, into dangerous, uncharted waters.
DANGERS Navigation by compass and stars alone; a crew ready to disobey their captain	**WHO** **CHRISTOPHER COLUMBUS** and about 90 crew **WHERE** across the Atlantic Ocean, which covers 20% of the Earth **WHEN** August 1492 to March 1493 **HOW** sailing ships called the *Niña*, the *Pinta* and the *Santa Maria* **DISTANCE** 3,200 km (1,990 miles) **WHY** to find a new trade route to the Far East
BACKGROUND	The lands of China and India were rich with spices, but Europeans could only reach them by making a long, arduous land journey east across deserts and mountains.

Columbus knew the Earth was round. He decided to try to reach the far *east* of the globe by heading round to the *west* – the opposite direction to other sailors. Instead he arrived in the Americas.

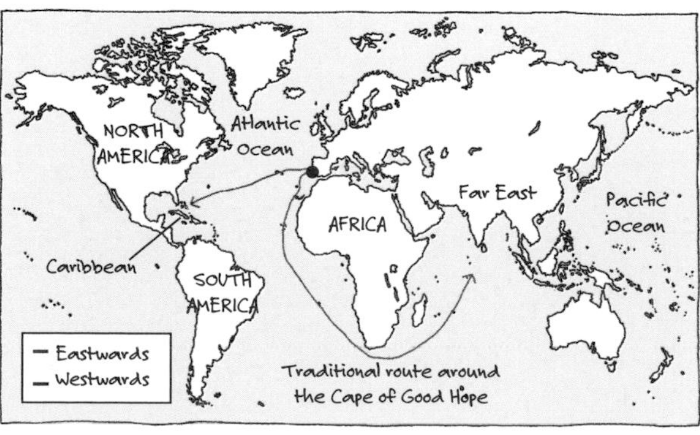

In this 19th-century painting by the artist Antonio Cabral Bejarano, Columbus boards the ship at the port of Palos in southern Spain. A crowd gathers on the shore to watch.

VOYAGE TO NEW WORLDS

☞ The three small wooden boats set sail with no idea what awaited them ...

On 3 August 1492, after years of trying to raise money for his voyage, Columbus was ready to sail from Palos, Spain, heading west into uncharted waters. It would be an exciting but dangerous journey and Columbus would have to use all his knowledge and skill. If he found a new route to the Far East he would become rich, powerful and famous – but would he and all his crew survive?

↑ In Columbus's time, most people knew the world was round, not flat. But nobody had tried to head west around the globe because the journey would take too long.

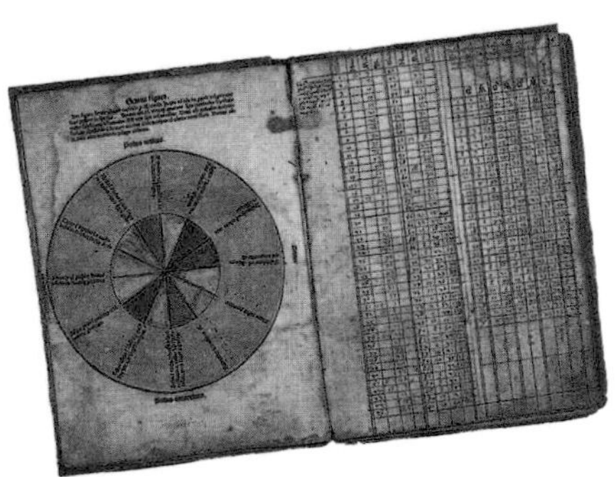

↑ Out at sea, with no sight of land, it can be very easy to become lost. Even with the stars, a compass and his charts, Columbus was still sometimes not sure if he was going the correct way.

↑ Columbus's journey helped change how people pictured the continents. This globe from around 1522 is one of the first to show the Americas.

↑ Columbus's ship, the *Santa Maria*, was about 25 m (80 ft) long, while the other two ships were only 15 m (49 ft) long. Life on board was cramped.

12 August Columbus stops in the Canary Islands off the north coast of Africa to pick up supplies and make repairs.

30 September The crew have been at sea for eight weeks – the longest journey ever known without sight of land.

7 October A lookout mistakenly cries "Land!" from the crow's nest, but it's a false alarm.

8 October Nearly two months have now passed since the crew last saw land and the sailors are frightened.

9 October Columbus lies to the crew about the distance they have traveled to keep them calm.

10 October The sailors are very close to disobeying their captain, Columbus. They no longer trust him and are ready to mutiny! They want to go home.

FEARS! BE PREPARED

Could you ...

>> sleep on a hard wooden deck?

>> eat food filled with maggots?

>> cope with feeling seasick?

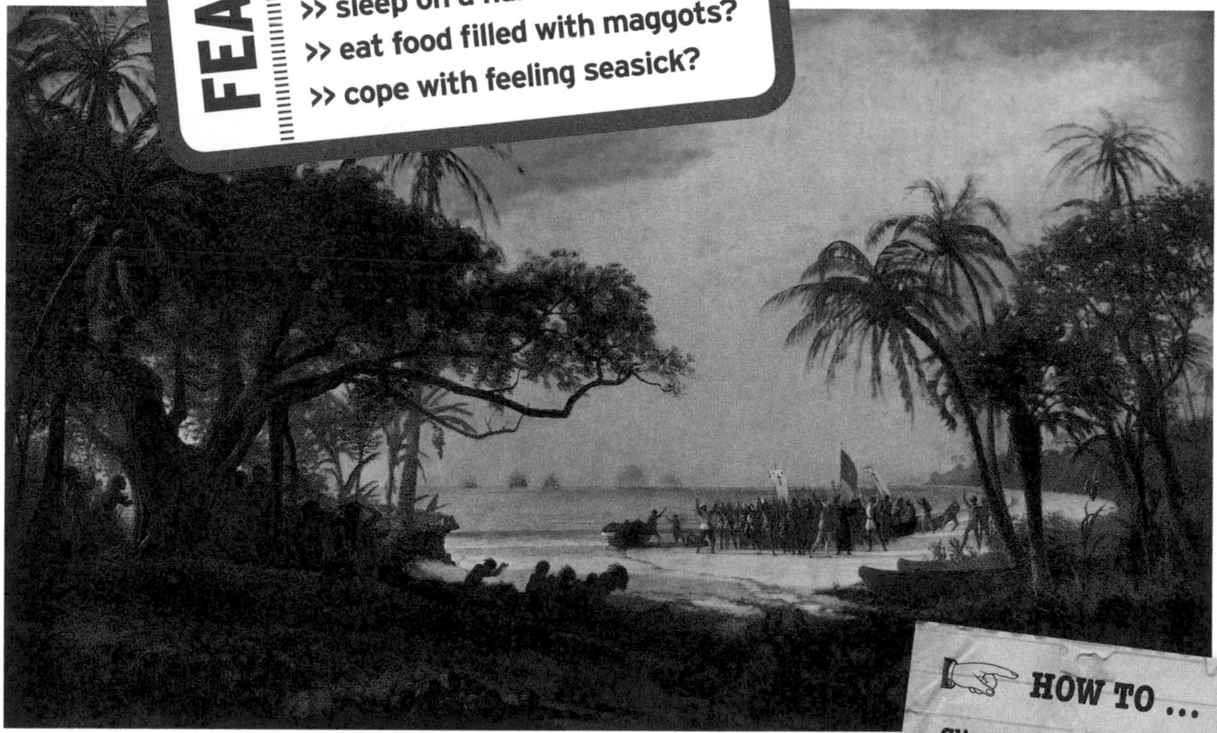

↑ When Columbus arrived, he wrote: "At daybreak great multitudes of men came to the shore. They came to the ship in canoes, wrought in a wonderful manner."

12 October In the middle of the night another cry rings out from the crow's nest. This time the lookout is right! The Europeans land at an island in the Caribbean and name it San Salvador, which means "holy saviour." Europeans and Native Americans meet there and begin to trade. The day is still celebrated as Columbus Day in the United States.

24 December While exploring islands near by, the *Santa Maria* is wrecked on rocks, but luckily the crew survive and manage to escape.

16 January Columbus and his men head for home in the *Niña* and *Pinta*, but the ships are separated along the way.

15 March Finally, the *Niña* and *Pinta* both arrive back at Palos in Spain, the port they had set sail from seven months before. Columbus is given a hero's welcome, and announces that he has reached the east! He doesn't realize that he has been to the Americas.

HOW TO ...

Climb the Rigging to the Crow's Nest

The best place to look out for land and enemies is the crow's nest – a basket at the top of the rigging.

1. Always climb on the side of the ship facing the wind, so you're blown into the ropes.
2. Imagine you are crawling! Pull yourself up, one arm at a time.
3. Don't look up, don't look down! Look straight ahead to keep your balance.

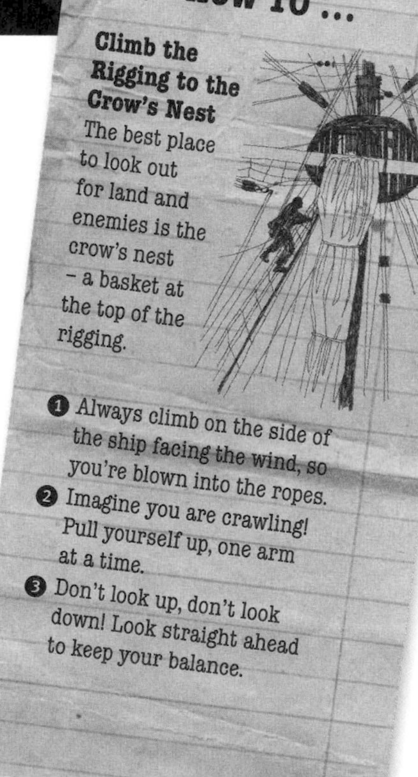

ACROSS THE SEA OF DARKNESS

THE CHALLENGE

 To sail east across an unknown ocean, battling extreme winds and unpredictable sea currents.

DANGERS

Deadly storms; wild winds and treacherous rocks; violent attacks by local Arabs

WHO **VASCO DA GAMA** and a crew of 150 men
WHERE around the coast of Africa into the Indian Ocean
WHEN July 1497 to September 1499
HOW with ships called the *São Gabriel*, the *São Raphael* and the *Berrio*
DISTANCE about 9,600 km (6,000 miles)
WHY to find a trade route by sea to the Far East

BACKGROUND

Christopher Columbus and Vasco da Gama explored routes to the East around the same time. Explorers would achieve fame and fortune if they expanded trade with this rich region.

Previous sailors had reached the tip of Africa from Europe but they were too frightened to travel further. With the wind in his favor, da Gama made it all the way to India.

NAME: Vasco da Gama
BORN: 1460s
DIED: by the age of 55
NATIONALITY: Portuguese
JOB: explorer and navigator
REMEMBERED FOR: exploring the east coast of Africa, sailing further than anyone else before.

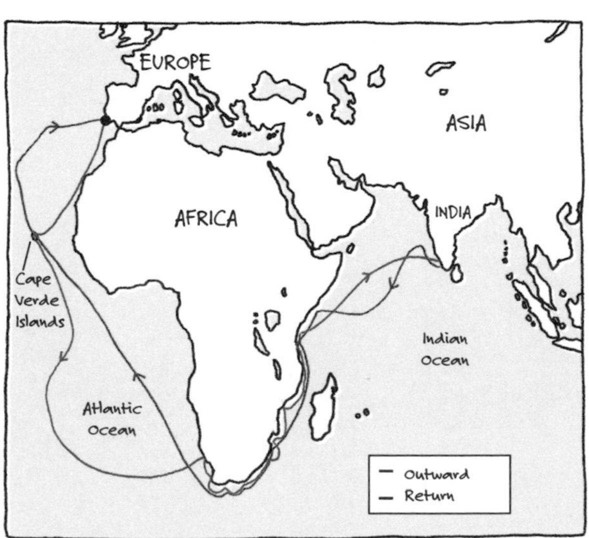

The Portuguese designed new ships, called caravels, with huge canvas sails to give them a better chance of sailing the long distances needed to get from Europe to India. Da Gama made his voyage of discovery in caravels like these.

S. pantaliao

Pedrafonsso daguiar

Diogo frz correa por feytor de cochim

lionarda

Dom luis coutinho Ramiro

S. Jeronimo

Dom vasq da gama

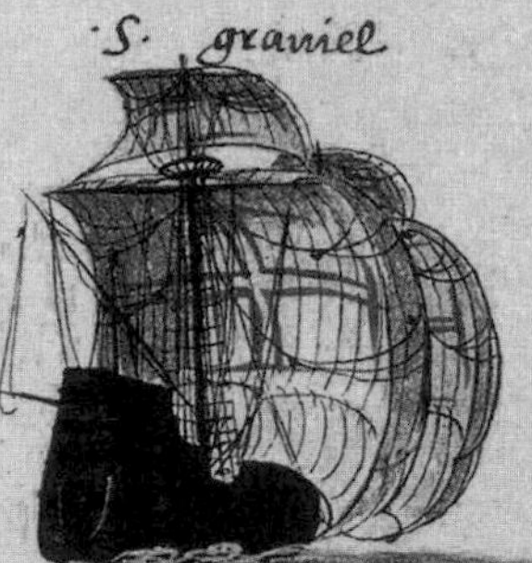

S. graviel

gil matoso

João lopez perestrello

Bate cabello

Ruy de castanheda

Antonio do campo com temporal esgarrou & mes perdido foy Invernar ẽ hũas jlhas na costa de Mellinde sem saber onde estaua

gil frz

leytoa noua

francisq da cunha das jlhas terceyras,

☞ Would the crew survive their extreme journey into the Indian Ocean?

↑ Da Gama took the latest navigational instruments with him. An astrolabe measured the height of the sun and the changing positions of the stars.

When Vasco da Gama set sail from Lisbon, Portugal, on 8 July 1497, few people believed that he would survive the raging seas around the African coast south of the equator, or ever make it back home. Da Gama was only 26, but was already a highly ambitious and ruthless captain. He was also a skilled navigator with a few tricks up his sleeve.

Instead of heading straight down the deadly African coastline, after loading supplies at the Cape Verde Islands he swung out into the mysterious Atlantic Ocean, known as the Sea of Darkness. This allowed his ships to be blown along by favorable winds and reach the tip of Africa in just four months – a record time. A previous expedition had taken one year!

But it was not all plain sailing. Terrified at entering the unknown waters of the Indian Ocean, the crew threatened to overthrow their captain and make him turn back. As da Gama traveled up the east African coastline, the local Arabs attacked.

↑ After da Gama's journey, the shape of Africa was redrawn. This 16th-century map shows some of the places he visited along the east coast of Africa.

↑ This woodcut shows Vasco da Gama inside a rich palace after arriving in India. He is handing a letter from the King of Portugal to the ruler of the area.

DANGER!

WATCH OUT

Deadly threats ...

- **>> waves wash you overboard**
- **>> your ship smashes into rocks**
- **>> you start to starve**
- **>> you get a mystery disease**

↑ Da Gama brought back spices from India including cinnamon, cloves and black pepper. In the 15th century, these spices were as valuable as gold and jewels.

↑ This holy vessel is rumoured to contain gold from da Gama's travels.

In return, he looted their ships. To make matters worse, his sailors began to suffer from scurvy, a dreadful disease, which would kill them if not treated.

Finally, on 20 May 1498, ten months after leaving home, da Gama made it to India. But there were still problems. The Indians were insulted by the cheap strings of coral and fishermen's hoods given to them as gifts, as well as by da Gama's arrogant behaviour. Eventually he departed with gems, gold, silk and exotic spices to bring home.

The journey back was treacherous. Desperate to escape, da Gama ignored local knowledge about the monsoon rains and was caught in storms and headwinds, slowing down his ships. Scurvy took hold again and over half of his crew died. He set fire to one of his ships because it was no longer needed. It took him more than a year to get back.

Nevertheless, da Gama returned a hero. He rode in triumph through the streets and was named Admiral of the Indian Ocean. He had achieved what had been thought impossible, finding a sea route to Asia. This epic journey helped to turn Portugal into one of the most powerful kingdoms in the world.

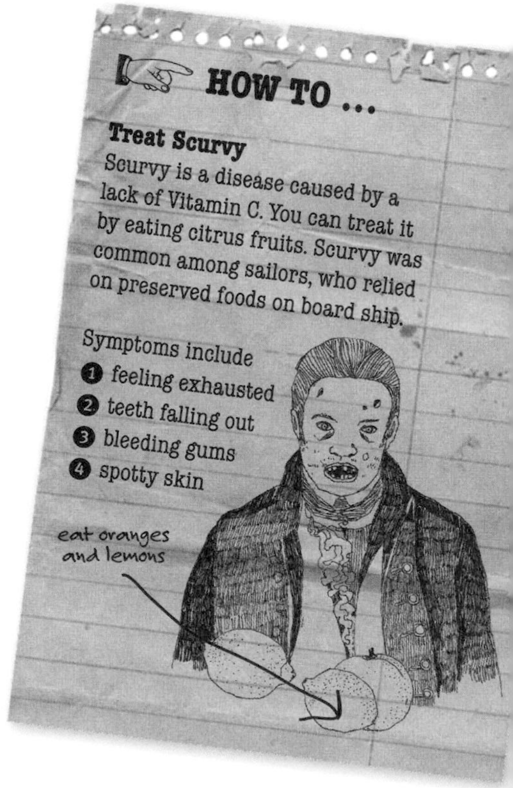

ROUND-THE-WORLD CHALLENGE

THE CHALLENGE	 A grueling sea journey around the world, sailing further than anyone else before.
DANGERS Thunderstorms and gales; a desperate crew ready to mutiny; violent local people	**WHO FERDINAND MAGELLAN** and a crew of 237 men **WHERE** from Spain in Europe to the Spice Islands, Southeast Asia **WHEN** 1519 to 1522 **HOW** with five long-distance wooden sailing ships **DISTANCE** over 67,000 km (42,000 miles) **WHY** to find a new sea route to the Far East
BACKGROUND	Although Magellan was Portuguese, he fell out with his country and became an explorer for Spain. Both countries wanted to trade in valuable spices from the Far East to increase their wealth.

When Magellan set off for the Spice Islands, Portugal controlled the sea route east, so he headed west toward South America. No European had sailed around the tip of this continent before.

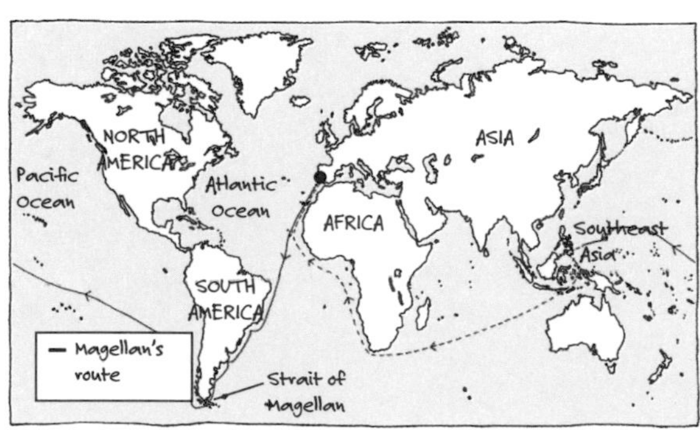

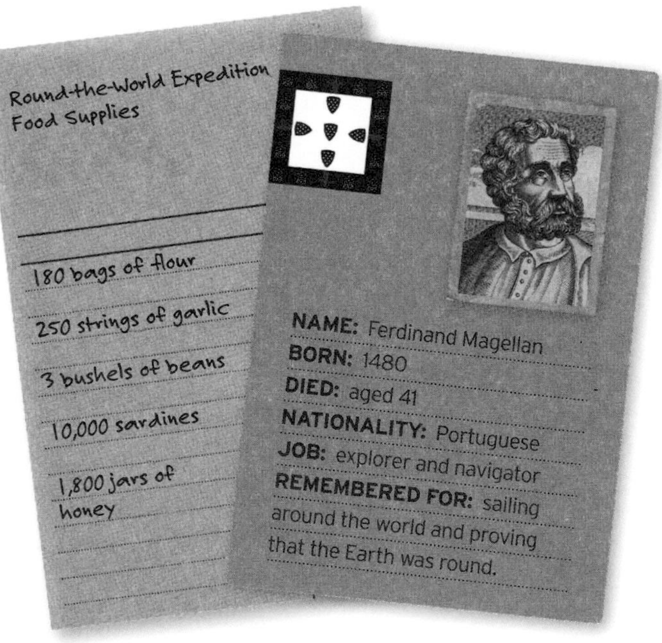

This map of the Spice Islands was drawn by Antonio Pigafetta, who traveled with Magellan as his assistant. He kept a journal during the expedition.

Machian.

Mutir.

Pulonghai :-

Mare.

Mallucque :-

Tadore.

Caiu gomode: Cest larbre de Girofle. :-

ROUND-THE-WORLD
CHALLENGE

☞ What terrors lay in the unknown waters around South America?

↑ Magellan's crew brought back spices including nutmeg and cloves. The cargo of cloves alone was so valuable that it paid for the whole trip and still made a profit.

↑ Magellanic penguins live off the coast of Chile in South America and are named after the explorer. Magellan recorded seeing small birds here that swam in the sea.

In September 1519, Ferdinand Magellan left the port of Seville in Spain in a daring bid to find a sea passage round South America to the Spice Islands in the Far East. No one knew if it was possible, and perhaps Magellan himself wouldn't have attempted the journey if he had realized how inaccurate his maps were. He estimated that on reaching the tip of South America, it would take him three days to sail to the East. It took him over three months!

During the long voyage, the crew faced terrible hardships. The men ran out of food and were forced to eat rats. While thunderstorms raged, they saw what looked like fire at the top of the ships' masts, caused by a weather effect known as St Elmo's fire. This filled the superstitious sailors with fear. Some of them mutinied and Magellan executed the leaders.

↑ Magellan set sail with five ships called the *Trinidad*, *Santiago*, *Concepción*, *San Antonio* and *Vittorio*. The *Vittorio* (shown above) was the only one to make it back home.

ROUND THE WORLD
Follow the voyage of Magellan and his crew around the world from 1519 to 1522. By opening up a sea route from Europe to the Spice Islands in the East, Magellan helped to turn Spain into a powerful trading nation.

1519 September — Magellan and a crew of 237 men set sail from Spain in five ships.

1520 April — On the South American coast, a mutiny breaks out. Magellan stops it.

1520 November — Magellan loses two ships but finally makes it to the Pacific Ocean.

1521 March — After sailing 11,000 km (6,835 miles) further than he thought, Magellan arrives in the Philippines.

A painting shows the battle on the island of Mactan, where Magellan was killed.

Finally, in March 1521, after a year and a half of sailing, Magellan landed at a group of islands that are today known as the Philippines. But disaster struck. On a trip to the island of Mactan with 50 men, Magellan found himself surrounded by 1,500 angry and armed local people. In a fierce battle, Magellan was hit by a poisoned arrow and killed.

Even though the remaining crew were desperate and afraid, they made it to the Spice Islands further south two months later. Here they picked up a valuable cargo and headed home with a new captain, Juan Sebastián Elcano. In September 1522, three years after setting off, they arrived back in Seville. They had traveled all the way around the world in an incredible feat of endurance. Although Magellan never completed the journey, by sheer determination he had found his sea passage through the tip of South America, now named the Strait of Magellan, and proved that the Earth was round.

After Magellan died, Captain Juan Sebastián Elcano took command of the journey home. Elcano was a ship's master on the expedition, helping with navigation. He was not the first choice for captain but as respect for Elcano grew, he took charge and sailed the *Vittorio* home.

1521 April	**1521 May**	**1521 June**	**1521 December**	**1522 May**	**1522 September**
Magellan is killed on the island of Mactan along with eight of his men.	A third ship is abandoned because there are not enough crew members.	The crew make it to the Spice Islands in two remaining ships, but one later springs a leak.	The last ship heads for home loaded with spices. Elcano is now captain.	The ship reaches the tip of South Africa. It is almost halfway home from the Spice Islands.	Elcano arrives in Spain with only 17 other sailors left on board but they have sailed around the world.

INTO THE PACIFIC

THE CHALLENGE	 A perilous journey of discovery through raging seas to distant new islands in the southern Pacific Ocean.
DANGERS Howling winds; wild waves; suspicious islanders; diseases from poor diet	**WHO ABEL TASMAN** and 110 crew **WHERE** around Tasmania, New Zealand, Tonga and Fiji **WHEN** August 1642 to June 1643 **HOW** in his tall sailing ships *Heemskerck* and *Zeehaen* **DISTANCE** about 28,900 km (18,000 miles) **WHY** to claim trading lands for the Dutch East India Company
BACKGROUND	The Dutch East India Company was a powerful organization that controlled much of the commerce around the Indian and Pacific Oceans. It was always on the lookout for new business opportunities.

While working for the Dutch East India Company, Tasman was sent to investigate reports of a fabled southern continent, today called Australia. He ended up sailing around the islands of Tasmania and New Zealand to the south instead.

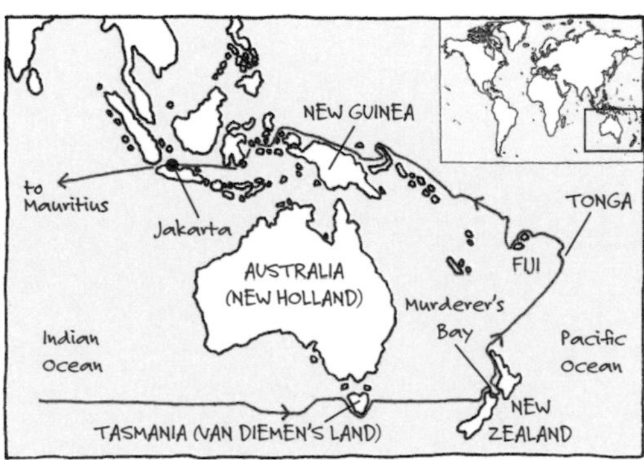

To the front of this scene are islanders in a canoe. In the distance, Tasman's ships are launching smaller boats to find drinking water. After the Maori became violent and attacked, Tasman named the area Murderer's Bay.

INTO THE PACIFIC

The two tall ships left port destined for the stormy southern seas ...

HOW TO ...

Raise the Sails

Raising the sail on a ship helped it to pick up speed. Tall, square-rigged ships such as Tasman's needed a large crew to hoist the sails quickly.

1. Make sure the ship is moving.
2. Steer it into the wind.
3. Untie the sails and carefully unfurl them.
4. Pull on the halyard, which is the rope that raises the sails.
5. Tie up the halyard when the sails are taut and not flopping about.

↑ In this illustration, small Tongan canoes welcome Tasman's tall ships. Tonga is a group of islands in the southern Pacific Ocean that stretch in a line over 800 km (500 miles) long.

↑ A portrait thought to be of Abel Tasman and his family.

By the time Abel Tasman set off on his dramatic voyage to discover a legendary southern continent, he was already an experienced sailor. The governor-general of the Dutch East Indies, Anthony Van Diemen, asked Tasman to lead the expedition, believing that his captain would find fertile land for farming and silver and gold to mine. But would this adventure into the unknown turn out as Van Diemen hoped?

On 14 August 1642, Tasman set sail from Jakarta in Indonesia. After picking up fresh water and other supplies in Mauritius, an island off the east coast of Africa, he turned south to catch the wind. Before long, the weather worsened. Wind howled, fog loomed and waves raged. The crew were afraid, but Tasman's expert navigation by compass helped keep everyone safe.

Then on 24 November, after the storms cleared, a lookout sighted land. Tasman named it Van Diemen's Land in honor of his boss. Crew members rowed ashore. They saw notches cut into trees like giant steps, which made them think huge people lived there, but no one stepped out from between the branches to meet them.

BE PREPARED

Could you ...

>> deal with a rebel crew?

>> sail into unknown stormy seas?

>> battle sickness and hunger?

The weather turned rough again and Tasman headed east. On 16 December, a lookout spotted land once more. The ship had arrived at New Zealand. This time the islanders, called the Maori, were waiting. The Maori had lived in New Zealand for about 400 years, and this was their first meeting with Europeans. They were deeply suspicious. They sailed out to Tasman's ship in a large canoe and attacked, killing four of his crew. The survivors fled for their lives.

Sailing northeast through more storms, Tasman arrived at the islands of Tonga and Fiji. Then, in June 1643, ten long months after setting off, he made it back to Jakarta. Van Diemen was disappointed that his captain had not found any riches, but today people recognize Tasman's incredible achievements. The island that was named Van Diemen's Land is now called Tasmania after the daring explorer!

↑ Tasmania is a large island off the south coast of Australia. The horseshoe bay in the distance, called Blackmans Bay, is one of the places where Abel Tasman landed on his journey of discovery.

Tasman's Journal
24 November 1642

In the afternoon, about four o'clock ... we saw the first land we have met with in the South Seas ... very high ... and not known to any European.

EXTRA

MEET THE MAORI PEOPLE

The Maori were the first people to settle in New Zealand. They arrived from nearby islands.

One Maori custom is the haka, a traditional group dance with feet-stamping and loud cries. It was often performed before a battle as a show of strength.

Some Maori people tattoo their bodies and faces with intricate designs to celebrate important events in their lives. The more tattoos a person had, the more they were respected.

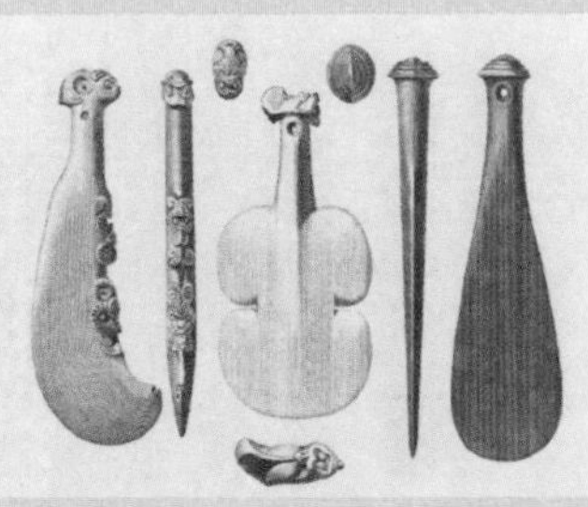

In the past, battles between Maori tribes were common. Many Maoris were expert warriors. They used short flat wooden clubs like these for fighting.

CHARTING THE SOUTH SEAS

THE CHALLENGE	 An epic three-year voyage, testing sailors to the limit in dangerous uncharted waters at the far south of the world.
DANGERS Extreme weather conditions; running aground; a leaking ship; dreadful diseases	**WHO JAMES COOK** and a crew of 96 scientists and sailors **WHERE** England to Tahiti and Australia in the southern Pacific Ocean **WHEN** August 1768 to July 1771 **HOW** in his 32 m (106 ft) square-sail research ship HMS *Endeavour* **DISTANCE** over 46,500 km (28,900 miles) **WHY** to make scientific observations and chart new lands
BACKGROUND	English scientists asked Cook to record information about the passage of Venus across the Sun. This rare event was best viewed from the island of Tahiti. Cook was also given a secret mission.

During Cook's voyage around the southern Pacific Ocean, also known as the South Seas, he spent six months mapping the coast of New Zealand and was the first person to travel along the east coast of Australia.

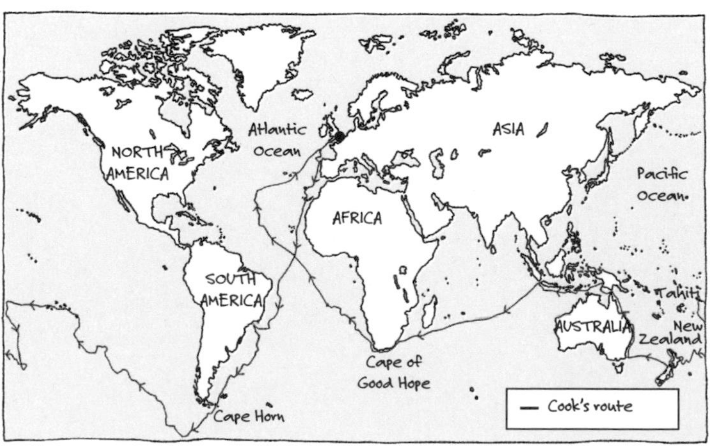

In this painting from 1775, Cook holds one of his own maps. His exploration of the South Seas and charting of new islands made world maps more accurate and detailed than ever before.

CHARTING THE
SOUTH SEAS

☞ What top-secret mission was Cook under orders to complete?

↑ During Cook's voyage, artists painted impressions of the scenes they saw. This picture shows a longhouse in Tahiti with banana and breadfruit trees on either side.

↑ This carving by the Maori people of New Zealand, called a tiki, was owned by James Cook. Tiki were valuable gifts and given only to people whom the Maori respected.

↑ Before Cook landed in Australia, Europeans had never seen a kangaroo. This painting by George Stubbs was based on a stuffed animal skin that Cook brought back.

On 25 August 1768, James Cook set sail from Plymouth, England, with an envelope in his pocket. He was told to open it only after he had carried out his observations of the planet Venus. Inside, there was a secret mission asking him to search for a new continent. In the 1700s, many people believed that a giant landmass stretched across the whole of the far south of the world and in places almost reached the equator. Would Cook find it?

↑ Inside a replica of Cook's ship HMS *Endeavour*. Up to 90 sailors slept here, below deck, in cramped conditions.

13 April 1769 Cook arrives in Tahiti after traveling for more than seven months. The crew have battled icy storms and tropical heat. The islanders row out to welcome the men.

3 June 1769 With their telescopes, Cook and an astronomer watch Venus pass across the Sun. They try to measure the distance between the two heavenly objects, but the results are mixed. Scientists explore the island, collecting information and making drawings of the plants and wildlife.

13 July 1769 HMS *Endeavour* leaves Tahiti and sails south. Cook is now following his secret orders. A lookout sights land but it turns out to be a bank of cloud. The weather grows so cold that the sailors' fingers freeze to the rigging. Cook decides to turn back.

DANGER!

WATCH OUT

Deadly threats ...

- >> malaria from mosquito bites
- >> sharks in the water
- >> dangerous coastline
- >> sunstroke on deck

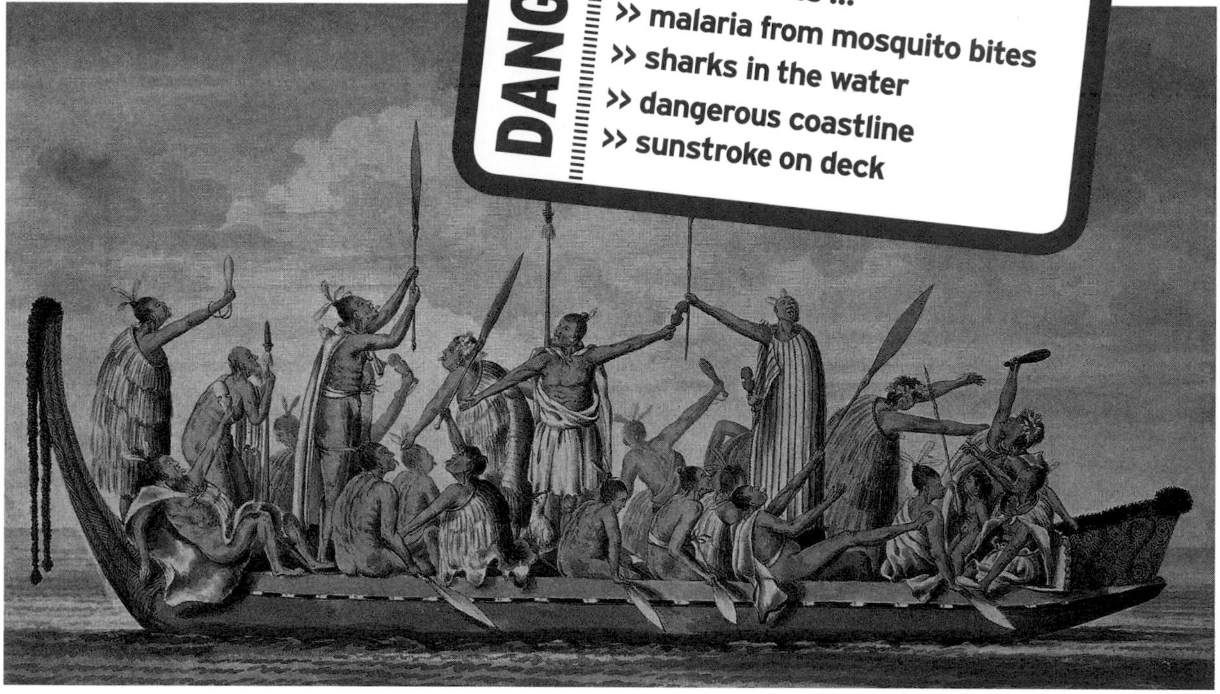

↑ The Maori people of New Zealand rowed out to Cook's ship in a war canoe. After a difficult start, Cook earned their respect and developed a friendship with them.

6 October 1769 The ship arrives in New Zealand. Could this be the new continent? Cook is not convinced. He maps the coastline and discovers the land is actually two islands.

19 April 1770 Cook drops anchor in Botany Bay, Australia, and his scientists collect hundreds of new plant specimens. Then, while sailing up the treacherous east coast, the ship smashes into a coral reef and springs a leak. Only expert sailing by Cook gets the ship out of disaster.

12 July 1771 After three years at sea, HMS *Endeavour* finally makes it back home to England.

James Cook never did find his giant continent because it didn't exist. But, unknown to him, he had sailed close to Antarctica. Although relatively small, it was named a continent in the 1890s. Cook made two other voyages of discovery in his lifetime, sailing a distance equivalent to traveling to the Moon! On these epic journeys, he discovered more of the Earth's surface than any other explorer who ever lived.

HOW TO ...

Steer with the Ship's Wheel

The ship's wheel is attached to the rudder underneath the boat. By turning the wheel you move the rudder and change the direction of the boat.

1. To turn portside, which means to the left, spin the ship's wheel to the left.
2. To turn starboard, which means to the right, spin the wheel to the right.
3. To keep a straight course, hold the wheel steady.

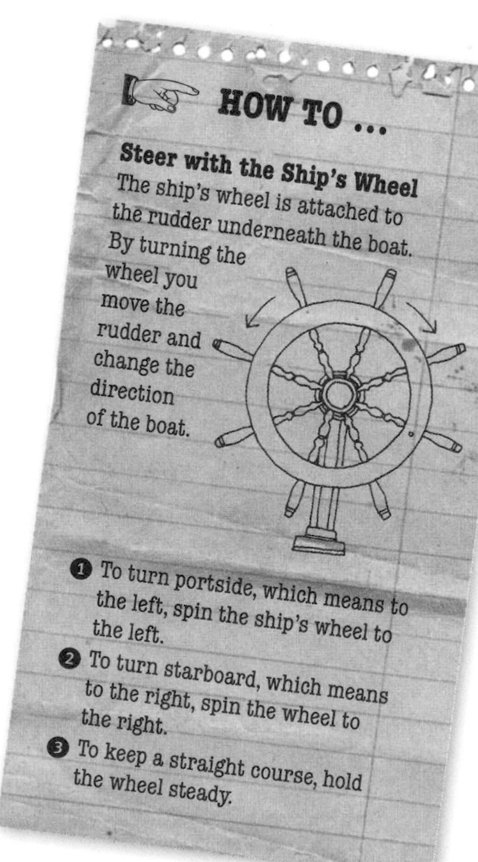

AN ASIAN ADVENTURE

THE CHALLENGE	 To spend over 20 years exploring the East, a daring feat never before attempted by medieval adventurers.
DANGERS Burning hot days; freezing cold nights; desert sandstorms; exhaustion	**WHO MARCO POLO** with his father, Niccolo, and uncle, Maffeo **WHERE** from Venice, Italy, to China and other parts of Asia **WHEN** 1271 to 1295 **HOW** on foot and by camel caravan, returning mostly by boat **DISTANCE** about 39,000 km (24,240 miles) **WHY** working for the Mongol emperor of China, Kublai Khan
BACKGROUND	Marco Polo's father and uncle had already made one trip to China, where they met the emperor Kublai Khan. He sent them home as his ambassadors and hoped that one day they would return.

Expedition to China
List of Supplies

- camels for carrying provisions
- horses to ride
- containers of water for the desert trek
- one month's supply of food

NAME: Marco Polo
BORN: 15 September 1254
DIED: aged 70
NATIONALITY: Italian
JOB: adventurer and writer
REMEMBERED FOR: providing the first detailed European account of life and culture in Asia.

No one is sure about the exact route Marco Polo took across Asia but in his writings he tells of traveling overland across high mountains and vast deserts until he arrives at Kublai Khan's court, north of modern-day Beijing.

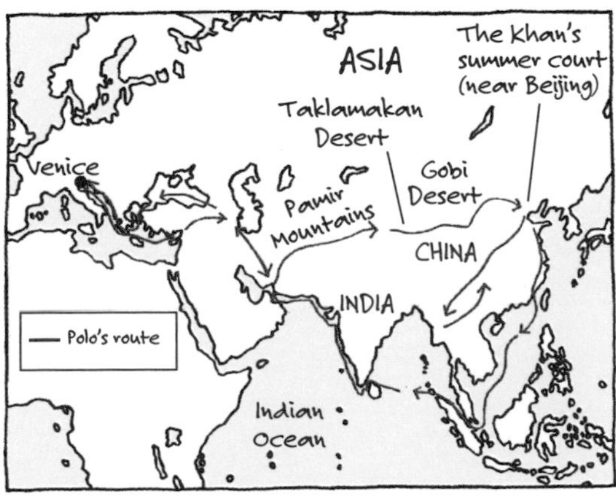

Marco Polo dressed in Tartar costume. The Tatars were a northern Asian wandering people, whom Polo may have met.

AN ASIAN ADVENTURE

What magical adventures lay in store for the young Marco Polo?

At the time of Polo's departure, Venice was a bustling port. Many boats left from here because it was an important center of trade between Europe and the rest of the world.

Kublai Khan was the ruler of the Mongolian Empire from 1260 to 1294. The empire included modern-day Mongolia and China, so Khan was also the emperor of China.

While writing about his time in the Pamir Mountains, Marco Polo described flocks of wild sheep with huge horns. Today, these animals are known as Marco Polo sheep.

At the age of 17, Marco Polo packed his bags and left home with his father and uncle to explore a strange new world thousands of miles away in the East. It was a place that people in Europe knew little about. They would find out, many years later, when Polo returned as a middle-aged man with a trove of almost unbelievable stories to tell.

In 1271, the family set sail from the port of Venice and headed south. They intended to travel much of the way by sea but were horrified by the flimsy boats offered to them when they reached the Asian continent, so they decided to make a dangerous and exhausting trek overland instead.

The journey took them through the Pamirs, a rugged mountain range with icy glaciers and forbidding high peaks. Today, this area is often called "the roof of the world." They crossed the vast Taklamakan and Gobi Deserts. Here, the days were burning hot and the nights freezing cold, with temperatures as low as -20°C (-4°F). Making it to the next waterhole was a constant challenge. In 1275, the Polos finally arrived at Kublai's summer court in northern China. They had been on the road for four years, traveling further than any Europeans before them.

With its gravel plains and shifting sand dunes, the Taklamakan Desert is a dangerous place. Its name in Turkish means "go in and you won't come out."

↑ The emperor Kublai Khan presents the Polo brothers with a gold tablet. This serves as their passport for a safe journey through the East.

Kublai welcomed the young Marco Polo and his family. For the next 17 years they worked for the emperor, who sent Polo on missions around China, India and parts of Southeast Asia. Polo later boasted that he explored "more of those strange regions than any man that was ever born." In 1292, the family finally decided to return home. They carried out one last task on their way, taking a Mongol princess to Persia, now modern-day Iran, so she could marry a prince there.

When Polo arrived home in 1295, Venice was at war. In 1298 he was imprisoned. In his cell, he told his adventures to another inmate who wrote them down. A book, known as *The Travels of Marco Polo*, was published. It became an instant bestseller. But the stories in it seemed so incredible that experts still wonder if they are true. Did Polo go to China at all? We shall never know the answer, but when confronted on his deathbed about his "lies," Polo replied, "I have only told you the half of what I saw."

→ *The Travels of Marco Polo* was translated into many languages, often with different titles. It was sometimes called "The Million." This is thought to refer to the number of exaggerated statistics and facts the book may contain.

EXTRA

WONDERS OF THE ORIENT

Marco Polo cataloged all kinds of wonders, never before heard of in the West.

While traveling, he described merchants who traded in rolls of the finest silk cloth. Only the Chinese knew the secret of silk-making at this time.

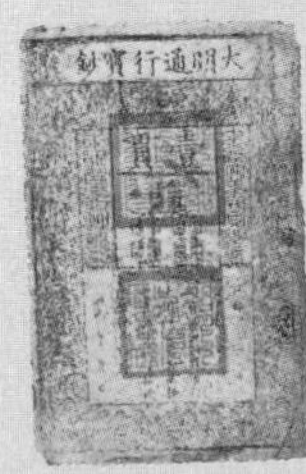

He also wrote about paper money, which merchants handed over for large transactions instead of heavy copper coins. Europe only started using paper money regularly in the 17th century.

The Chinese invented porcelain. They made it by heating kaolin, a type of clay, to high temperatures. Marco Polo describes porcelain bowls for sale on his travels.

GOLD RUSH IN FLORIDA

THE CHALLENGE	 To venture through dense swampland into an unknown part of North America, under attack by Native Americans.
DANGERS Getting lost; being ambushed by angry Native Americans; running out of food	**WHO HERNANDO DE SOTO** with 620 men and 223 horses **WHERE** from Florida to the Mississippi River and Gulf of Mexico **WHEN** May 1539 to May 1542 **HOW** on horseback, on foot and by boat **DISTANCE** 6,440 km (4,000 miles) **WHY** to search for gold and to claim land for the Spanish crown
BACKGROUND	De Soto had already found gold in South America but he was driven by rumours of more treasures in an area known at the time as "la Florida" in the southeast of the modern-day United States.

After sailing from Cuba, where he was governor, de Soto landed on the Florida coast. He marched inland, then headed west toward Mexico, setting up camp each winter along the way.

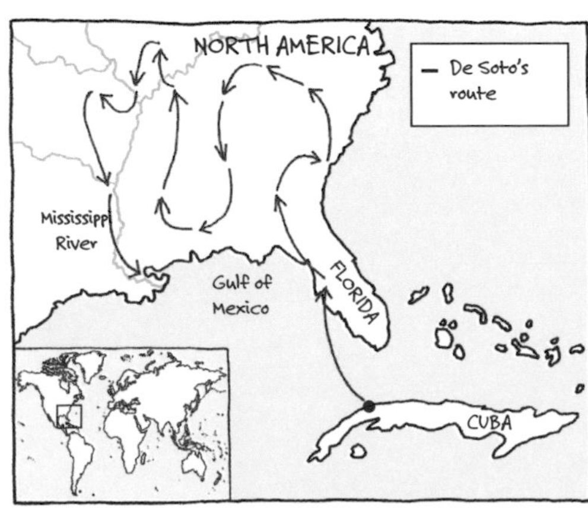

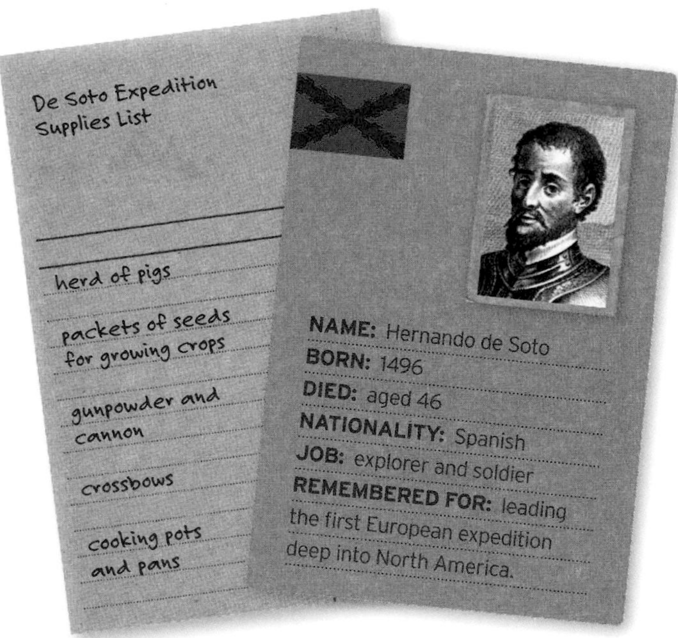

De Soto and his army of soldiers set up a temporary camp in the Florida wilderness. Parts of the Florida coastline are still covered with thick tropical swamps and wetlands.

GOLD RUSH
IN FLORIDA

☞ Would de Soto ever find the hoards of gold he was looking for?

When Hernando de Soto stepped onto the Florida shore with his army in May 1539, he meant business. He was already a successful conquistador, or warrior, who had defeated the Incas, the native people of Peru in South America. He had returned weighed down with gold and was hoping to find more. Imagine how the Native Americans must have felt when this strange-looking European stormed onto the land where they had lived for centuries. They were going to put up a fight.

For months, de Soto marched through muddy swamps and across high mountains. When he arrived at a village, he demanded food and men to guide him on. By 1540, he had made it into Choctaw territory, but here, a hostile chief lured him into a town and attacked. About 200 of de Soto's men were killed and many horses lost. In revenge, de Soto burned the town to the ground. Over 2,000 Native Americans died.

↑ Many different Native American tribes lived in North America. This is a Timacuan chief. The Timacuans covered their bodies with tattoos to show off their fighting achievements.

↑ This face is made out of shell and forms part of a pendant to wear around the neck. It was crafted by Native Americans who lived near the Mississippi River, where de Soto was traveling.

↓ This engraving shows the Choctaw attacking de Soto's men with bows and arrows. The battle with the Choctaw was one of the worst de Soto encountered.

HOW TO ...

Make a Dugout Canoe

The Native Americans used dugout canoes for hunting and fishing. It's one of the oldest types of boats ever made.

1. Find a tree trunk long and wide enough to sit in.
2. Strip off the bark and shape the outside with an ax and chisel. Make sure the canoe has a pointed end at the front.
3. Now hollow out the center so there is a place to sit. Finally, make the boat waterproof by smearing it with boiled tree resin.

De Soto crosses the Mississippi and is met by Native Americans in canoes.

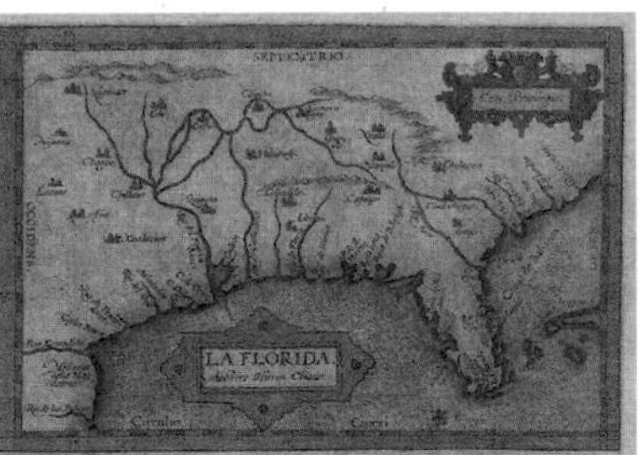

A map from 1584 showing Florida and a section of the surrounding lands. It is partly based on information from de Soto's travels.

In May 1541, he arrived at the banks of the Mississippi River. Convinced that riches lay hidden on the other side, his men built rafts, fought off more Native Americans and made it across. The party marched on and on but winter approached with no sign of any gold. After sitting out the season, weak and with few supplies, de Soto gave up and turned back.

De Soto died from a fever on the banks of the Mississippi River in May 1542. About 300 of his men struggled on and made it home to the Spanish colony of Cuba in 1543. They had been on the march for four years!

De Soto's gold was just a dream but he did become the first European to cross the Mississippi River. He will also be remembered for a more chilling reason. His army introduced diseases, including measles and chickenpox, to the Native Americans. This caused many of the natives to die and, in time, had a devastating effect on their population.

HISTOIRE
DE LA CONQUÊTE
DE LA
FLORIDE,
OU
Relation de ce qui s'eſt paſſé dans la découverte de ce Pays par Ferdinand de Soto.
Compoſée en Eſpagnol par l'Inca Garcilaſſo de la Vega, & traduit en François
PAR P. RICHELET.

Imprimé à Lille, & ſe vend :
A PARIS,
Chez JEAN MUSIER Libraire, Quai des Auguſtins. M. DCCXI.
Avec Approbation & Privilege du Roy.

Our knowledge of de Soto's travels is incomplete. Much of it comes from this book written by a survivor of the expedition. Archaeologists have also found pottery remains which may be connected to the journey.

TAMING THE WILD WEST

THE CHALLENGE	 A perilous journey of discovery across North America from east to west, over a harsh and varied landscape.
DANGERS Raging rivers; high rocky mountains; ice and snow; wild animals; exhaustion	**WHO MERIWETHER LEWIS** and **WILLIAM CLARK** **WHERE** St Louis, in the state of Missouri to Clatsop, Oregon **WHEN** May 1804 to September 1806 **HOW** by boat, on foot and on horseback **DISTANCE** over 14,485 km (9,000 miles) **WHY** to complete a study of the land and its resources
BACKGROUND	When US President Thomas Jefferson bought a large chunk of the United States in 1803 from the French, in a deal called the Louisiana Purchase, he wanted to find out about his new territory.

On the way to the west coast of the United States, Lewis and Clark traveled together. When heading back east, they split up at times to explore different areas.

Meriwether Lewis posed for this painting of himself in clothes given to him by the Shoshone tribe. The explorers met many different Native American peoples on their expedition.

☞ The US president leaned over and asked Meriwether to investigate ...

↑ This is a Blackfoot chief. Although Lewis and Clark developed friendly relations with over 30 Native American tribes, the Blackfeet were suspicious of the new owners of their land and their meeting ended in violence.

The new land bought by President Jefferson in 1803 toward the west of the United States was a complete mystery to him. Was it fertile for farming? Were there minerals to mine? And would the Native Americans who lived there be friendly? He would find out by sending an explorer, and he knew just the person for the job – Meriwether Lewis, his personal secretary. At the same time, Lewis could investigate whether there was an easy river route across the country, which would be valuable for transport and trading.

Lewis immediately got in touch with his old army buddy, William Clark, and they set up a team of 31 helpers. Calling themselves the Corps of Discovery, they headed up the long, winding Missouri River. The journey was punishing. Rather than paddling, the party often had to pull their boat along against the strong current with tow ropes. The winter was bitterly cold and ferocious bears were roaming the landscape.

↑ Conical basket hats woven from cedar-bark fibers were typical headwear among Native American tribes along the northwest Pacific coast. Lewis and Clark collected hats like these on their expedition.

↑ The upper Missouri River teemed with herds of buffalo.

DANGER!

WATCH OUT

for wild animals including ...

- **>> huge grizzly bears**
- **>> stampeding buffalo**
- **>> poisonous rattlesnakes**
- **>> infectious mosquitoes**

↑ The Corps of Discovery meet the Hidatsa tribe, who live along the Missouri River. Toussaint Charbonneau, the fur trapper husband of Sacagawea, acts as a translator.

The Corps also had to cross a section of the Rocky Mountains controlled by the Shoshone tribe. Without the tribe's help, it would be impossible to navigate the treacherous icy trail. Earlier, Lewis and Clark had met a fur trapper named Toussaint Charbonneau whose wife, Sacagawea, was a Shoshone. She made sure that her people provided horses and guides. After 11 exhausting days, the group stumbled out of the mountains, starving, freezing, but still alive. Lewis and Clark then canoed downriver, shooting rapids, finally reaching the west coast of the United States nearly two years after they had set off.

The journey back was hazardous too, but they made it home, complete with a treasure trove of information about the animals, plants, land and peoples they had seen. They also put an end to the idea that there was an easy river route all the way across the United States.

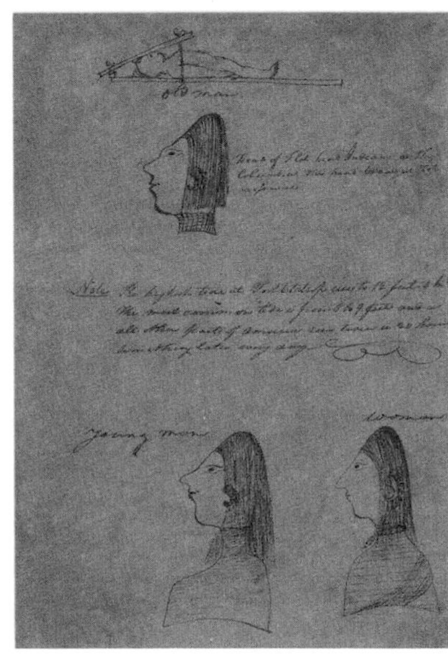

↑ Lewis and Clark kept detailed daily journals about their travels. Their writings filled eight volumes. Here they describe the old Native American practice of head flattening used by some west-coast tribes.

→ It is thought that this "spy glass" was carried by Meriwether Lewis to view animals in the distance. When fully opened, it reached 1.5 m (nearly 5 ft) in length.

COAST TO COAST

SECRET AFRICA

THE CHALLENGE	 To cross Africa by river, hacking through thick jungle and exploring areas never visited by Europeans before.
DANGERS Slimy swamps; terrifying rapids; sickness and hunger; ferocious wild animals	**WHO** **DAVID LIVINGSTONE** and a small team of porters **WHERE** the length of the Zambezi River in Central Africa **WHEN** November 1853 to May 1856 **HOW** on foot and by canoe **DISTANCE** about 8,050 km (5,000 miles) **WHY** to find a passage to the sea and open up trade in Africa
BACKGROUND	David Livingstone had already been exploring Africa for 13 years. In 1851 he discovered the lower part of the Zambezi River, the fourth-largest river in Africa. This inspired him to travel further.

Livingstone's 1853 journey took him from Cape Town in southern Africa to Luanda on the west coast. He then headed back east along the Zambezi River to the town of Quilimane.

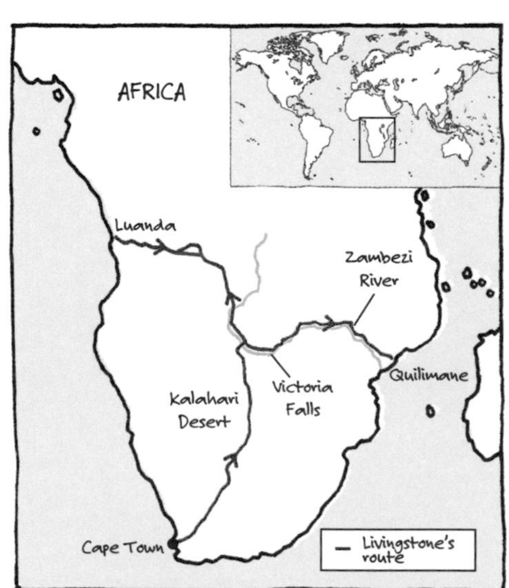

Throughout his life, Livingstone was committed to improving the lives of the African people. He strongly opposed the slave trade that existed at the time and spoke out angrily against it.

Would Livingstone make it out of the African jungle alive?

This boat's compass was used by David Livingstone on his journey.

During the early part of his life, David Livingstone worked as a missionary in Africa, trying to convert the local people to Christianity. But by the time he set off on his daring adventure into the heart of the jungle along the Zambezi River, he was more focused on exploring. Livingstone had a wife and young family back home in England. He knew the risks he was taking, but nothing was going to stop him.

Leaving Cape Town in 1853, he first walked north through the dry, dusty Kalahari Desert. He then turned west into thick swamp and forest. His friend Chief Sekeletu loaned 27 local men but the going was tough. Rain poured, the group ran out of goods to trade and had to abandon their canoes. Worse still, the area was rife with disease. When Livingstone arrived at the west coast after six months of journeying, he collapsed.

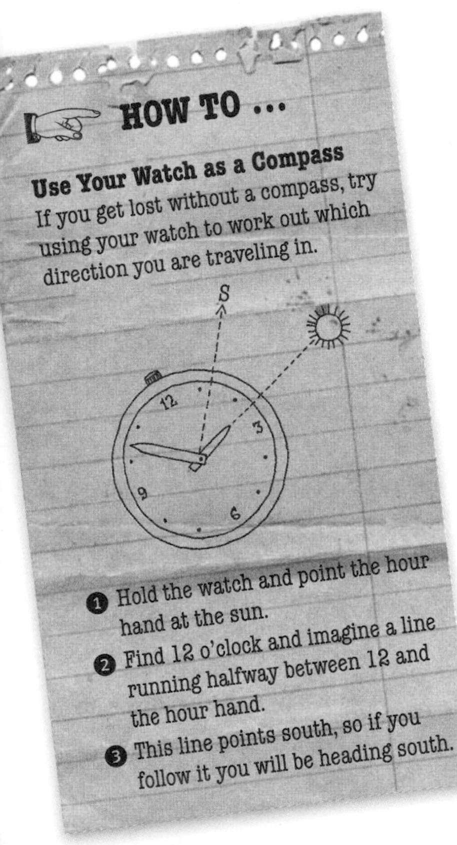

In this 19th-century painting by Thomas Baines, the brutal Kebrabasa Rapids crash down the Zambezi.

A LIFE IN AFRICA
Livingstone spent over 30 years exploring Africa. His discoveries filled in much information about this little-known continent. After 1866, he lost touch with the outside world until Henry Morton Stanley found him.

1841 March	1849 March	1851 August	1853 November
Arrives in Africa to work at a Christian mission but is disappointed by its lack of success.	Crosses the Kalahari Desert and finds Lake Ngami to the north.	Reaches the lower part of the Zambezi River and wants to investigate further.	Sets off on a mammoth expedition along the length of the Zambezi River.

FEARS! BE PREPARED

Could you cope with ...

>> insect bites all over your body?

>> fierce, snapping crocodiles?

>> a spear attack?

↑ The Victoria Falls plunge down the banks of the Zambezi River between Zambia and Zimbabwe. Their local name means "the smoke that thunders."

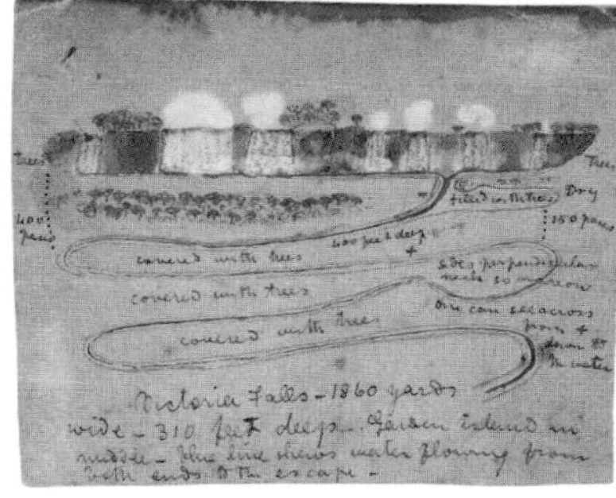

↑ During his adventure, Livingstone kept detailed records of the natural features he saw. He drew this sketch of Victoria Falls and noted the type of vegetation in the area.

Livingstone was offered a boat back to England but he refused to take it. He knew that if he left his men behind, they would be sold as slaves. Instead, he headed back into the jungle, this time going east along the river. Conditions were no better than before – rain fell, wild animals burst from the bushes and many local tribes were hostile. But Livingstone continued and made an amazing discovery. In November 1855, he arrived at a magnificent, thundering waterfall. He named it Victoria Falls in honor of the British queen.

Finally, in May 1856, he made it to the coast, becoming the first European to have crossed Africa from west to east. When Livingstone returned home to England, he had no idea how famous he had become. Not only had he survived his journey, but he had also been given a medal and was a national hero.

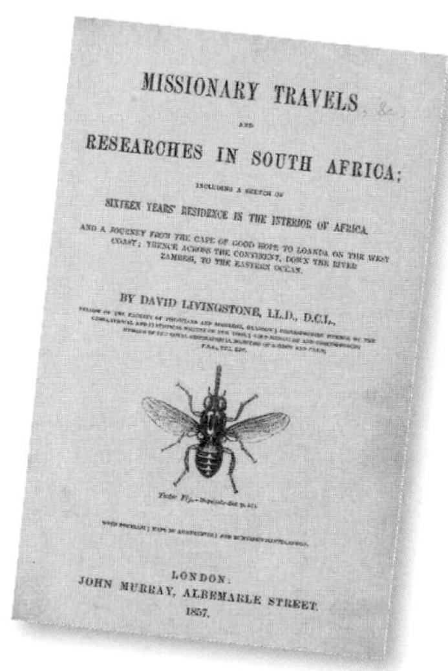

MISSIONARY TRAVELS

AND

RESEARCHES IN SOUTH AFRICA;

BY DAVID LIVINGSTONE, LL.D., D.C.L.,

LONDON:
JOHN MURRAY, ALBEMARLE STREET.
1857.

↑ In 1857, back in England, David Livingstone published a book called *Missionary Travels and Researches in South Africa* about his experiences. It became a huge bestseller.

1856 December	1858 March	1859 September	1866 January	1871 November	1873 May
Arrives back in England after crossing the African continent and finding Victoria Falls.	Returns to Africa and tries to sail up the Zambezi in a steamboat but gets stuck.	Discovers Lake Nyasa, the third-largest lake in Africa, running through Malawi.	Heads off on a journey to find the source of the River Nile and disappears.	Henry Morton Stanley finds Livingstone alive but ill in a town in Tanzania.	Livingstone dies, aged 60, in an African village after a lifetime of exploration.

SURVIVING IN THE AFRICAN JUNGLE

THE CHALLENGE	 A daring solo journey along river and through jungle into a remote part of Africa to meet a fearsome local tribe.
DANGERS Crocodile-infested waters; jungle traps; local tribes rumoured to eat human flesh	**WHO MARY KINGSLEY** and local guides **WHERE** Ogowé River in Gabon, West Africa **WHEN** December 1894 to October 1895 **HOW** by steamboat, canoe and on foot **DISTANCE** 110 km (70 miles) **WHY** to collect wildlife and study the local people
BACKGROUND	Kingsley had already made one pioneering trip to Africa before in 1893. She lived during Victorian times, when it was extremely unusual for a woman to travel long distances alone.

Sailing from England, Kingsley then paddled up the Ogowé River. She was the first European to climb Mount Cameroon in Africa.

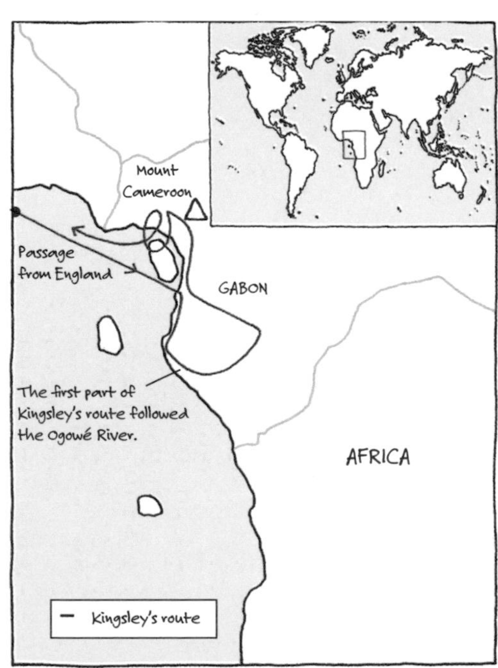

On her travels, Kingsley picked up curious objects, such as this power figure called a nkisi. According to tradition, you conjured up the figure's spirit to help solve problems by hammering in nails.

SURVIVING IN THE AFRICAN JUNGLE

Dressed in a long skirt and armed with an umbrella, Kingsley set off ...

Up until the age of 30, Kingsley lived at home. She educated herself by reading her father's books. When her parents died, she finally fulfilled her lifelong ambition to travel.

In December 1894, Mary Kingsley made her second trip to the west coast of Africa, setting foot in areas never visited by a European before. She was a truly remarkable woman, traveling alone without a tent, hacking through bush with a machete knife, and paddling her own canoe. She even fought off crocodiles by whacking them on the snout with her umbrella!

Kingsley's main goal was to meet the Fang people who lived along the Ogowé River deep in jungle country. This local tribe had a reputation for being fierce and were even rumoured to eat the flesh of defeated enemies. They certainly had never set eyes on a white European woman before. Luckily for Kingsley, the Fang people welcomed her. She lived among them, learned how to cook snake, traded cloth for souvenirs and got to know their customs.

Local guides, including Fang warriors, helped Kingsley find her way as she pushed further and further up the Ogowé River in her canoe.

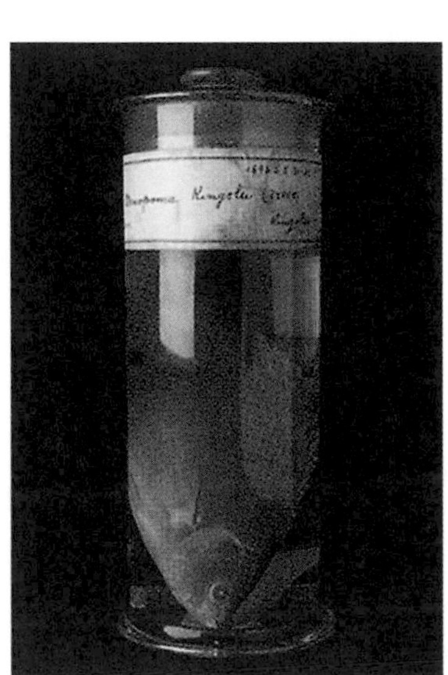

Mary collected fish specimens from the Ogowé River. She discovered three new species of fish that were named after her, including this one called *Ctenopoma kingsleyae*.

FEARS!

BE PREPARED

Could you ...

- >> wade through slimy water?
- >> let insects crawl over you?
- >> snack on snake stew?

HOW TO ...

Build a Jungle Shelter

You will need:

- long wooden pole
- shorter sticks
- machete knife
- vine rope
- large palm leaves

1. Set one end of the long wooden pole in the ground and the other in the forked branch of a tree.
2. Lean the shorter sticks against the pole to make a tent shape. Tie them on with the vine rope.
3. Use more vine rope to create a framework between the sticks. Then weave palm leaves in and out to make a covering.

← Kingsley took this photograph of Fang warriors. As well as guns, Fang men used wooden spears and iron-tipped arrows to hunt buffalo and antelopes.

↓ This photograph appeared in Kingsley's book *Travels in West Africa*. She stayed in traditional houses built from tree branches and straw.

During her stay, Kingsley had many hair-raising adventures. One day while exploring, she fell into an animal trap lined with 12-inch spikes, but survived. Another time, she was woken up by a dreadful stench in the hut where she was sleeping, only to discover a human hand, three big toes and other body parts in a bag hanging from the ceiling! Kingsley took it all in her stride.

In October 1895, Kingsley returned home. She wrote a book about her experiences called *Travels in West Africa* and became an instant celebrity, touring the country to encourage respect for the African way of life. Kingsley made one last trip back to Africa. Sadly, she died there at the age of 38 but her wild adventures were never forgotten.

Kingsley wrote

"It's at these times you realise the blessing of a good, thick skirt."
... when she fell into a spiked animal trap

↑ One of Kingsley's supplies was quinine. This medicine was used to treat malaria, a deadly tropical disease passed on by the bite of an infected mosquito.

THE HIGHEST MOUNTAIN

THE CHALLENGE	 To become the first people to climb to the top of the highest mountain in the world: to conquer Mount Everest.
DANGERS Bitterly cold winds; freezing temperatures; sheer cliff faces; deep cracks in the ice	**WHO EDMUND HILLARY** and **TENZING NORGAY** **WHERE** Mount Everest in the Himalaya, Asia **WHEN** 12 April 1953 (Base Camp) to 29 May 1953 (summit) **HOW** on foot with bottled oxygen **DISTANCE** Mount Everest is 8,848 m (29,029 ft) high **WHY** to stand on the highest point on the surface of the Earth
BACKGROUND	Many people had tried to climb Mount Everest before, including the British explorer George Mallory, who disappeared on a ridge close to the summit in June 1924. He may have been on his way down!

Mount Everest is the highest peak in the Himalaya, a huge mountain range stretching across southern Asia that includes most of the world's highest peaks.

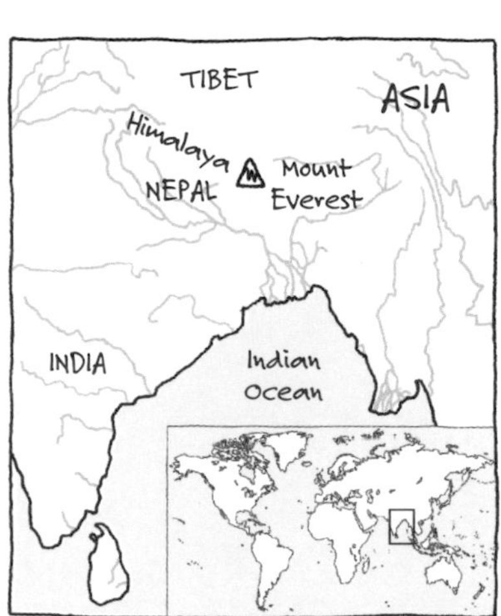

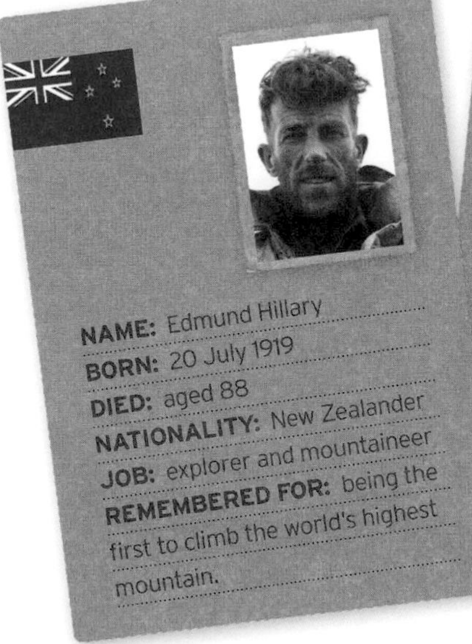

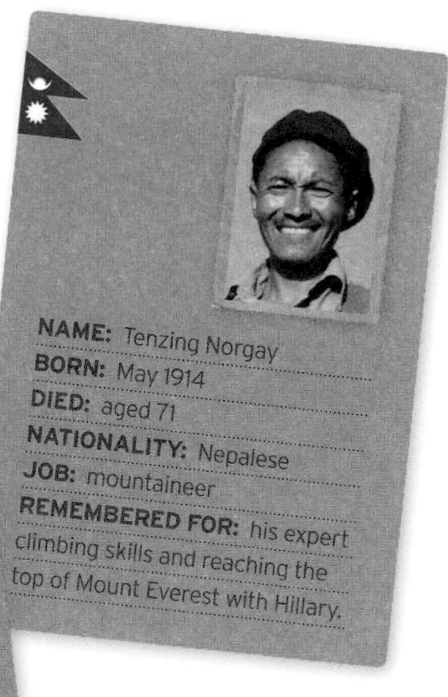

→ Hillary checks Tenzing's oxygen equipment before they push higher up the mountain.

THE HIGHEST MOUNTAIN

☞ Would Hillary and Tenzing be the first people to reach the top of Mount Everest?

↑ This is the route Hillary and Tenzing took up Mount Everest in 1953 from Base Camp. They traveled through the deadly Khumbu Icefall and along the South Col to reach the summit.

↑ All the climbing started from Base Camp. Tents were pitched here on the stony ground inside a ring of jagged ice.

↑ Near the top of Mount Everest is an area known as the Death Zone. Here the air becomes so thin that climbers usually need extra oxygen to breathe properly and survive. Above is the oxygen equipment that Hillary and Tenzing carried on their backs.

Long before Edmund Hillary and Tenzing Norgay met for the first time in 1953 at the base of Mount Everest, they had both shared a passion for conquering the world's highest mountain. By the time they became climbing partners, they were highly experienced mountaineers who knew the extreme challenges and terrible dangers of this colossal mountain well.

Hillary developed his climbing skills in the Southern Alps in New Zealand. In 1951, he explored a new route up the southern face of Everest, climbing the Khumbu Icefall. This river of ice, with its sheer crevasses (deep wide cracks), is one of the most dangerous stages in the journey to the summit.

As a boy, Tenzing lived in the shadow of Mount Everest among the Sherpa people. In the 1930s, he worked as a porter carrying supplies on several failed expeditions to reach the top of the mountain. In 1952, he was part of a Swiss team that made it to the South Col, a desolate windswept ridge past the Khumbu Icefall. Tenzing and another team member struggled on, using bottled oxygen to help them breathe, before finally giving up about 300 m (980 ft) from the summit.

In April 1953, the British expedition set up Base Camp below the Khumbu Icefall. The team set up eight other camps along the route to the South Col so that they could haul up supplies in stages and have places to rest. Group members including Hillary made a path through the icefall over several days. The porters followed with all the heavy equipment over several weeks. Incredibly, there were no accidents along the way.

From the South Col, a pair of climbers called Tom Bourdillon and Charles Evans made an attempt to reach the top. They came extremely close to achieving their goal but were forced to turn back with about 100 m (330 ft) to go when their oxygen began to run out and bad weather set in. They headed back wearily, having stood higher on the mountain than any humans before them. Now, it was Tenzing and Hillary's turn. They were the expedition's last chance for success.

↓ Expedition members cross a wide crevasse by laying down a metal ladder. The team had only one ladder, so they carried it with them from one deep crack to the next. It was slow, hard work.

DANGER!

WATCH OUT

for these perils ...

- >> falling into a deep crevasse
- >> collapsing from exhaustion
- >> being caught in a blizzard
- >> freezing to death

EXTRA

TEAM AND SUPPLIES

Over 400 people were involved in the expedition but a much smaller team completed the main part of the climb.

Here you can see members of the main climbing team. At the front are the porters and guides, Sherpa people who lived in the local area.

The Sherpas carried over 8,000 kg (17,600 lbs) of equipment in 473 boxes up the mountainside. Each item inside the boxes was numbered and listed.

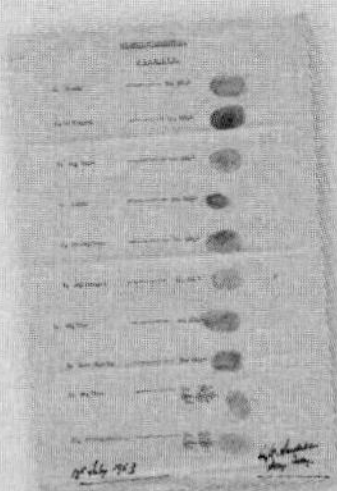

As proof of payment for their work, the Sherpas placed inked thumbprints next to their name and the amount on a list.

Would Hillary and Tenzing be the first people to reach the top of Mount Everest?

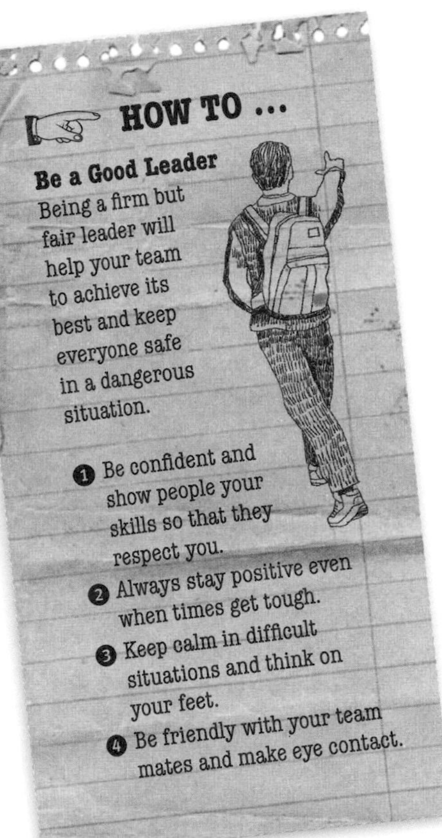

↑ During the climb, the mountaineers used tree trunks dragged up from lower valleys by the Sherpas as platforms to cross deep crevasses.

↑ At times in the journey, the climbers were confronted by huge walls of ice. They climbed up wobbly rope ladders to get to the top.

On 28 May, a five-man team helped Hillary and Tenzing set up Camp Nine, 8,500 m (27,890 ft) up the mountain. This was to be the last camp before the summit. The pair spent a night inside their dangerously pitched tent, barely able to sleep. They breathed bottled oxygen and ate tinned sardines, drinking lots of liquids to beat the terrible thirst they were suffering.

At 6.30 am, 29 May, they stepped outside into the bitter cold. Hillary's boots had frozen solid and took two hours to thaw. Then they began to climb with heavy rucksacks. By 9 am, they had reached the South Summit. They were now about 160 m (520 ft) from the top of Mount Everest. From here, they followed a knife-edge ridge with a huge drop on either side. If they fell it would mean certain death, so they took each step carefully. At the end of the ridge there was a 12 m (40 ft) high cliff face. Hillary somehow climbed up the rock and snow, hoping it would not collapse beneath him. Tenzing followed. Today this cliff face is known as the Hillary Step.

At about 11.30 am, the two men reached the top of the mountain. They looked down at the valleys and peaks spread out far below. They were standing on the highest point of the Earth's surface – on top of the world. They had done it!

Hillary and Tenzing spent just 15 minutes at the summit. The New Zealander pulled out a camera that he had kept warm inside his shirt and took a famous photo of Tenzing. Tenzing dug a hole in the snow and left sweets as a Buddhist offering to the gods. Hillary placed a cross given to him by the British commander of the expedition, Colonel John Hunt, inside the hole. Then they both made their way down from the summit while Colonel Hunt came up to meet them with hot soup.

↑ In this well-known photograph, Tenzing Norgay stands on the top of Mount Everest. He holds up an ice ax with the flags of the United Kingdom, Nepal, the United Nations and India tied on.

News that the expedition was a success reached the UK on 2 June 1953 – the day Elizabeth II was crowned queen. Hillary was knighted, and later went on to explore the Antarctic. Tenzing was given the George Medal but preferred a quieter life. Meanwhile, the world wondered who had reached the summit of Everest first. Eventually, Tenzing revealed that it was Hillary but the bond between the two men was so strong that for many years, neither would say.

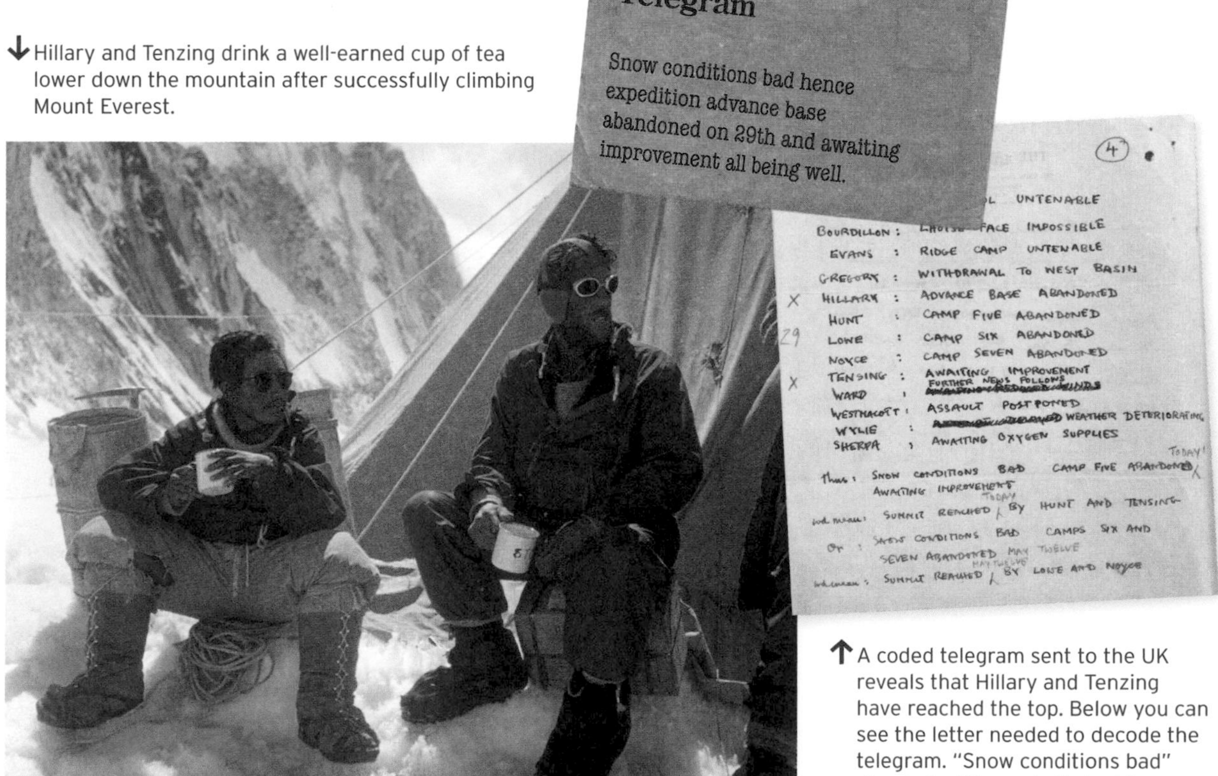

Telegram

Snow conditions bad hence expedition advance base abandoned on 29th and awaiting improvement all being well.

↓ Hillary and Tenzing drink a well-earned cup of tea lower down the mountain after successfully climbing Mount Everest.

↑ A coded telegram sent to the UK reveals that Hillary and Tenzing have reached the top. Below you can see the letter needed to decode the telegram. "Snow conditions bad" stands for "Everest climbed."

ALONE ON TOP OF THE WORLD

THE CHALLENGE	 To climb Mount Everest, the world's highest mountain, alone and without extra oxygen to help with breathing.
DANGERS Snowstorms; thick mists; collapsing snow; difficulty breathing	**WHO REINHOLD MESSNER** **WHERE** Mount Everest in the Himalaya, Asia **WHEN** 18 August 1980 (Base Camp) to 20 August 1980 (summit) **HOW** on foot **DISTANCE** Mount Everest is 8,848 m (29,029 ft) high **WHY** to test the limits of human endurance
BACKGROUND	In 1978, Messner successfully scaled Mount Everest with a climbing partner. They used no bottled oxygen, a feat never achieved before. The journey inspired him to return alone and try a different route.

Since the 1960s, Messner has scaled peaks in the Alps in Europe, the Himalaya and the Karakoram Range in Asia, and the Andes in South America. He often takes routes that have never been tried before.

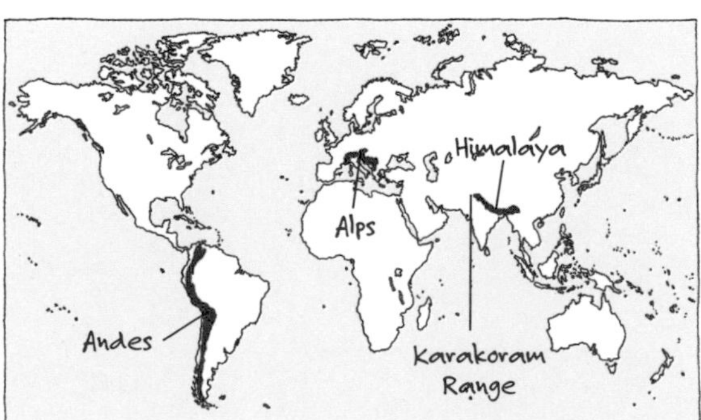

Mount Everest sits on the border between Nepal and Tibet in southern Asia. In 1980, Messner scaled the north face of Everest, including a steep gorge no one had climbed before.

ALONE ON TOP OF THE WORLD

☞ Alone, with his rucksack and tiny tent, Messner began the long climb ...

↑ Many people think that Reinhold Messner is the greatest mountain climber of all time. He began climbing, aged five, with his father.

Messner said

"I was in continual agony; I have never been so tired as on the summit of Everest that day. I just sat there oblivious to everything ... I was physically at the end of my tether."

↑ At the top of Mount Everest, Messner discovered a tripod from a previous expedition. He took this photo of himself by standing his ice ax in the snow and screwing his camera to it.

↑ A valley fills with mist on the slopes of Mount Everest, making it difficult for Messner to decide which way to go.

When Reinhold Messner left Base Camp on 18 August 1980, heading for the summit of Everest alone, he had already spent several weeks up in the mountains, getting used to the thin air and preparing himself mentally for the lonely climb. He decided not to take ropes to steady himself or ladders to cross crevasses. He would not communicate with the outside world. If anything went wrong, he would rely on himself.

The first part of the climb was treacherous. As he approached the North Col, a pass on the way to summit, the snow gave way and he fell into a crevasse. It was night-time and pitch black. He managed to switch on his headlamp and find a ledge to scramble onto and climb out. The journey passed without more accidents, but there were other things to worry about.

BREAKING RECORDS

In 1986, Reinhold Messner became the first person to climb the world's 14 highest mountains. These peaks are all in the Himalaya or the Karakoram Range. They are all higher than 8,000 m (26,000 ft). Here's how he did it.

1970	1972	1979	1980
Climbs Nanga Parbat, the world's ninth-highest mountain.	Reaches the top of Manaslu in the Himalaya by an unknown route.	Climbs K2 in the Karakoram Range, the world's second-highest mountain.	Stands on the top of Mount Everest, the highest mountain in the world, having climbed solo.

Messner climbed during the monsoon season when the weather often changed rapidly. Soon, the mists rolled in, the wind began to howl and a snowstorm raged. He waited out the storm inside his tent. With the freshly fallen snow also came the threat of an avalanche – a whole river of snow that could cascade down the mountainside at any time, burying him alive.

The last leg of the journey was grueling. Leaving his tent and rucksack to pick up on his return, Messner continued with only a camera and ice ax. He moved at a snail's pace. The air became so thin that his throat hurt to breathe. He was completely exhausted and stopped every 15 or so paces to rest.

At about 3 pm on 20 August, Messner made it to the top. He had completed the journey in just three days. Other explorers usually took a month. It was an amazing feat of endurance and speed, and he had achieved it by himself.

HOW TO ...

Survive an Avalanche

Getting caught in an avalanche is extremely dangerous and often life-threatening. Follow these tips to help you survive.

1. Do your best to stay on top of the snow. Move your arms like you are swimming front crawl.
2. If you are half-buried, kick the snow with your legs and dig down with your hands to get out.
3. If you are neck-deep, dig around you as quickly as you can.

FEARS!

BE PREPARED

Could you face ...

>> not talking to anyone for days?
>> feeling cold, sick and dizzy?
>> being too tired to move?

← Wearing a thick woolly hat and wrapped in a scarf to protect his face from the cold, Messner stands in front of the mighty mountain he conquered.

1981	1982	1983	1984	1985	1986
Climbs Shishapangma, the lowest of the 14 peaks, from the north side.	Conquers three mountains in one year – Kangchenjunga, Gasherbrum II and Broad Peak.	Follows a partially new route up Cho Oyu, the world's sixth-highest mountain.	Climbs Gasherbrum I and Gasherbrum II without returning to Base Camp in between.	Takes a new route up Annapurna during bad weather and heavy snowfall. He also climbs Dhaulagiri.	Completes the feat by climbing Makalu and Lhotse, two peaks next to Mount Everest.

ADVENTURES IN THE DESERT

THE CHALLENGE	 A daring trek across a windswept desert in the Middle East, fraught with danger from warring tribes.
DANGERS Wild sandstorms; fierce heat; the threat of violence; being caught as a spy	**WHO GERTRUDE BELL** **WHERE** the Arabian Desert in the Middle East, western Asia **WHEN** December 1913 to April 1914 **HOW** by camel train **DISTANCE** over 2,300 km (1,430 miles) **WHY** a passion for exploring the Arab world
BACKGROUND	Bell had already made several journeys to the Middle East before this one. Her first trip from 1899 to 1900, a camel trek around the Near East, gave her a love of traveling and the Arab peoples.

Bell's circular journey took her from Baghdad in present-day Iraq to Damascus in Syria. She then headed south through the harsh Arabian Desert to the oasis town of Hail. After being imprisoned there, she made it back to Baghdad.

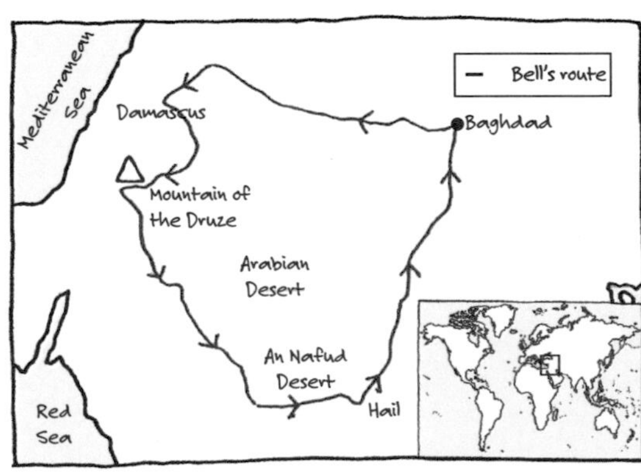

As well as being an explorer and writer, Bell was a keen archaeologist. Here she is standing in front of her tent on a dig to excavate the ruins of the ancient city of Babylon, in present-day Iraq.

ADVENTURES IN THE DESERT

☞ Bell set off into the desert on the most dangerous journey of her life ...

↑ This photograph of Gertrude Bell taken in 1900 in front of a monument shows her sitting astride a horse. Although practical, riding a horse this way was unusual for the time – most women still rode side-saddle.

↑ Bell used a tape measure like this one to survey the landscape.

↑ In 1921, Winston Churchill (a future British prime minister) asked Bell to attend a conference in Cairo, Egypt, about the Middle East. She was the only woman to do so.

↑ Gertrude Bell's camel train outside the city walls of Hail.

It took a huge amount of courage for Gertrude Bell to trek into the Arabian Desert on 16 December 1913. Not only was she entering a harsh landscape with an extreme climate, she was walking into an area where rival tribes were fighting for power. She was also a lone woman traveling in the Arab world at a time when it was very rare to do so. But no one needed to worry, Bell had enough guts and determination for ten people.

The British government asked Bell to collect information for them on the area but offered her no protection. She did it anyway. Leaving Damascus (in modern-day Syria), she went south among the Druze people. Although she spoke Arabic, the journey was hair-raising and at times violence threatened.

→ Bell took photographs to document the people, buildings and landscape of the Arab world. This photograph shows the courtyard of a house in Hail.

FEARS!

BE PREPARED

Could you cope with ...

>> the sun beating down on you?

>> sandstorms raging around you?

>> having gunshots fired at you?

↑ This desert castle in present-day eastern Jordan was built in the 8th century. Gertrude Bell visited the castle during her journey.

Her next challenge was the An Nafud, a desert where violent winds could whip up the red, clay-like sand in an instant, making progress difficult. On 26 February 1914, Bell finally arrived at the oasis town of Hail in present-day Saudi Arabia. Here, much-needed food and water were available. She may have thought her troubles were over, but she was promptly arrested by anti-British leaders. During an 11-day imprisonment, Bell made notes on the political situation, and after the leaders let her go, she hotfooted it to Baghdad. She had been the first European woman to visit Hail for over 20 years.

Bell returned to England and soon after, in July 1914, World War I broke out. The information she had collected proved very useful. The Arabian Desert trek was Bell's last great journey but it wasn't her last great achievement. When the war ended in 1918, she helped draw up boundaries for the new countries of the Middle East. Despite her early death at the age of 57, she will always be remembered as the Desert Queen.

Bell wrote

"I find it catching at my heart again as nothing else can, or ever will, I believe, thing or person." ... about her love of the Middle East

EXTRA

TRAVELING THROUGH ASIA

Over the years, other women with a spirit of adventure have made their names traveling through Asia.

At the age of 58, Isabella Bird (1831–1904) trekked from Baghdad to Tehran after a lifetime of other journeys.

Freya Stark (1893–1993) journeyed to remote parts of Persia, today Iran, never visited by Westerners before. She also explored the southern Arabian Desert.

Dervla Murphy (born 1931) cycled through Iran, Afghanistan, Pakistan and India, often alone and in dangerous situations. She has written about her travels.

IN SEARCH OF ANCIENT KINGDOMS

THE CHALLENGE

To cross the hostile shifting sands known as the Rub' al Khali (Empty Quarter) in southern Arabia.

DANGERS

Dying of thirst and starvation; suffering from extreme exhaustion; getting lost

WHO **WILFRED THESIGER** and his Bedouin traveling companions
WHERE Empty Quarter, Arabian Peninsula, western Asia
WHEN October 1946 to February 1947
HOW by camel and on foot
DISTANCE over 15,000 km (9,320 miles)
WHY to explore new lands and experience traditional ways of life

BACKGROUND

Although in the 1930s British explorer Bertram Thomas had become the first known European to cross the Empty Quarter, large areas of this desert still remained unexplored.

The Empty Quarter covers most of the southern third of the vast Arabian Peninsula. It is the largest sand desert in the world. On his 1946 journey, Thesiger covered the east of the desert. Later, he traveled around the west.

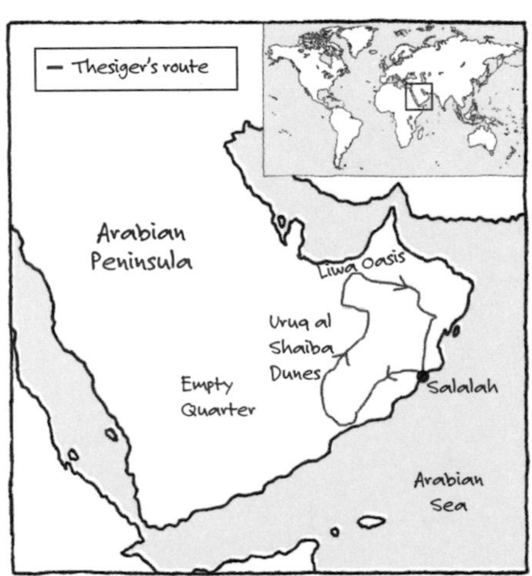

Wandering Bedouin tribesmen bin Kabina and bin Ghabaisha were Thesiger's loyal companions on several of his journeys.

While traveling, Thesiger dressed like the local tribespeople and followed their customs. Here he is wearing an Arab-style shirt and headdress. He is holding a stick to guide his camel.

☞ What drove Wilfred Thesiger to explore the bleak deserts of Arabia?

↑ This traditional curved Arabian dagger, known as a khanjar, belonged to Wilfred Thesiger. He wore it belted around his waist inside the sheath.

↑ Giant sand dunes stretch across parts of the Empty Quarter.

Throughout his life, Wilfred Thesiger was driven to explore lands untouched by modern civilization. In the 1940s, when he made his most famous journeys, such places were hard to find. The Empty Quarter, a hostile desert stretching across the southern Arabian Peninsula in western Asia, fitted the bill. Here he could escape contact with the outside world. The desert was home to wandering Bedouin tribes, and Thesiger was fascinated by their traditional way of life. He decided to experience the desert the same way as they did.

In October 1946, he set off from the coastal town of Salalah, in Oman, with his camel and six Bedouin tribesmen. Traveling north, the group endured burning hot sun during the day – temperatures in the Empty Quarter can reach as high as 56 °C (133 °F). At night it was freezing cold. Eventually, the group arrived at the Uruq al Shaiba, a long chain of mountainous sand dunes, reaching up to 215 m (700 ft) high.

↑ Traveling by camel was the best way to cross the dry, dusty desert. These hardy animals can walk long distances without water.

Thesiger said

"To others my journey would have little importance ... It was a personal experience, and the reward has been a drink of clean, tasteless water. I was content with that."

→ On all of his journeys, Thesiger took photographs of the local people, buildings and landscape. He kept his camera in a goatskin bag to protect it from the sand.

Climbing the dunes was exhausting work and, to make matters worse, supplies were running low. Thesiger and his companions struggled on, dying of thirst and starvation. When they finally made it to the Liwa Oasis on the northern edge of the desert, where food and water were plentiful, they were extremely relieved. In February 1947 Thesiger arrived back in Salalah after five months of traveling.

Thesiger made more journeys into the Empty Quarter and in 1949 crossed the Umm al Samim (Mother of Poisons), a treacherous area of salty quicksand. No European had visited this quicksand or the Liwa Oasis before. He later wrote a book about his desert adventures called *Arabian Sands*. His writings taught us much about the Bedouin way of life and inspired a generation of future travelers. Maybe they will inspire you to explore too.

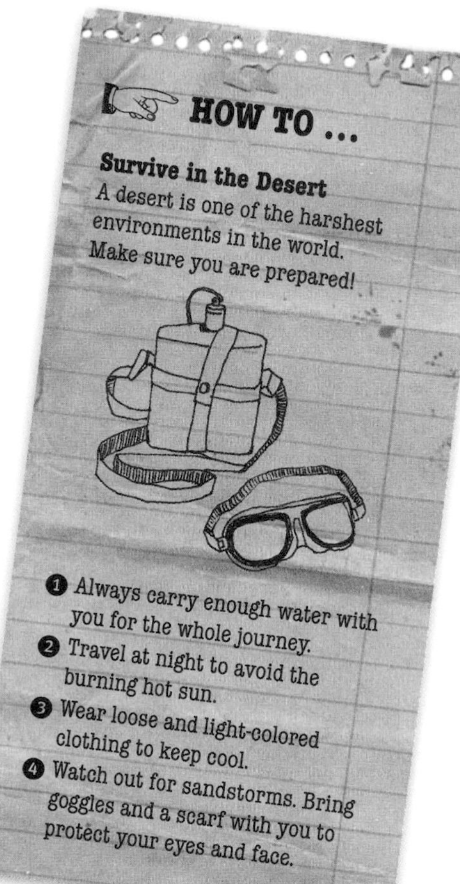

HOW TO ...

Survive in the Desert

A desert is one of the harshest environments in the world. Make sure you are prepared!

1. Always carry enough water with you for the whole journey.
2. Travel at night to avoid the burning hot sun.
3. Wear loose and light-colored clothing to keep cool.
4. Watch out for sandstorms. Bring goggles and a scarf with you to protect your eyes and face.

↓ Thesiger left us with over 35,000 photographs as a record of his travels. This photo from 1955 shows the construction of a guesthouse from reeds in Iraq.

PIONEER OF THE SKIES

THE CHALLENGE	 Crossing the dangerous Atlantic Ocean, the second-largest ocean on the planet.
DANGERS Freezing conditions; strong winds; mechanical failures; no radio contact	**WHO AMELIA EARHART** **WHERE** from Newfoundland, Canada, to Northern Ireland **WHEN** May 1932 **HOW** in a single-engined Lockheed Vega 5B airplane **DISTANCE** 3,270 km (2,030 miles) **WHY** to be the first woman to cross the Atlantic Ocean solo
BACKGROUND	Earhart was passionate about flying. She also wanted to make sure women had the same chances in life as men. She created a special club for female pilots to help them take up flying as a job.

Amelia Earhart had over 3,270 km (2,030 miles) of water to cover in the cramped cabin of her plane. With no radio for the next 15 hours, she had to navigate her route east over the Atlantic Ocean carefully.

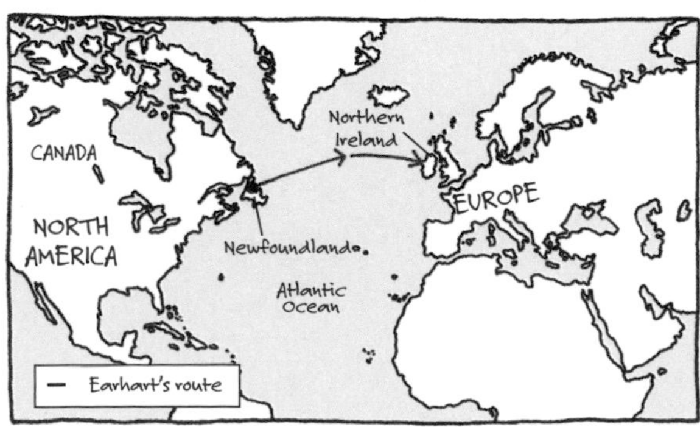

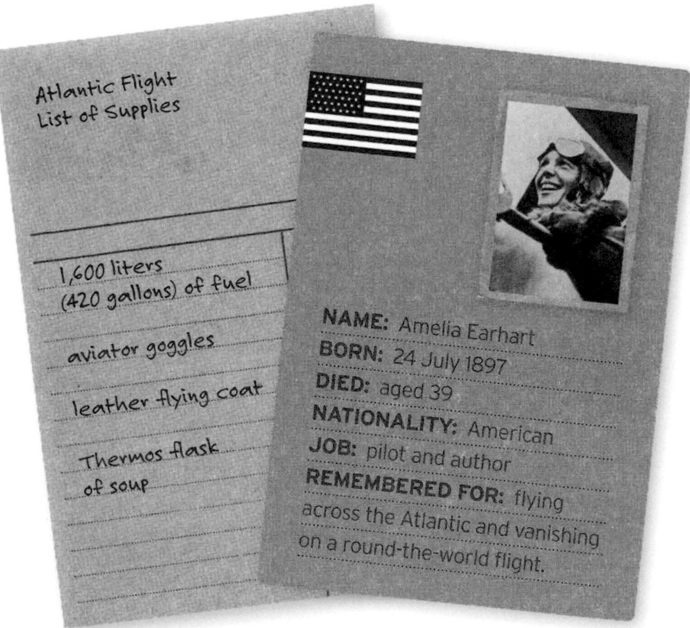

Earhart stands in front of her Lockheed Vega 5B airplane. As well as breaking flying records, she also took part in airplane races, which made her popular with the public.

HAMILTON STANDARD
PROPELLER CORPORATION

PIONEER OF THE SKIES

☞ Earhart flicked the switch and the propellor whirred into action ...

↑ This powder compact and mirror was part of Earhart's flying kit. She was always keen to look her best in front of the cameras after a flight.

By the time Amelia Earhart made her daring solo flight across the Atlantic Ocean in May 1932, she was already famous for being the first woman to have flown across the same ocean as a passenger. Despite being an experienced pilot, she had then felt as "useful as a sack of potatoes." This time she wanted to show the world that it was her in charge of the controls, and earn the respect of her fellow pilots.

She set off at 7.12 pm from a small airport in Newfoundland, Canada, knowing that her journey was extremely risky. Flying non-stop through the night for just under 15 hours, she battled high winds and dense fog. Her fuel tank leaked, flames shot out of the engine and ice covered the wings of her plane. At one point she fell into a tailspin, just managing to pull out of it and avoid crashing into the waves.

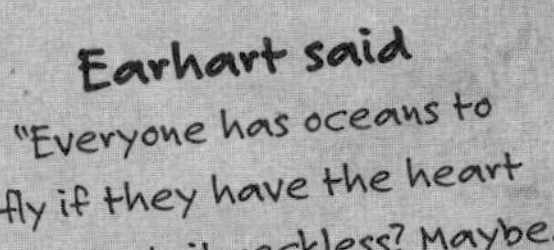

↓ Earhart's single-engine Lockheed Vega airplane was bright red. She called it her "little red bus." It is now on display in a US flight museum in Washington, D.C.

↑ Earhart sits in the cockpit of one of her planes. On her Atlantic crossing a flight instrument called an altimeter broke and she was unable to tell how high she was in the sky.

FEARS!

BE PREPARED

Could you face ...

- **>> flying solo through a storm?**
- **>> the plane rattling and shaking?**
- **>> being out of radio contact?**

↑ Dressed in her leather flying suit on top of her Lockheed Vega, the crowd cheers Earhart after a successful landing.

Earhart had no idea where she was when she finally touched down in a farmer's field in Northern Ireland, but she had done it. Not only had she become the first woman to pilot a plane across the Atlantic Ocean single-handedly, but she had also flown further without stopping than any woman before.

Amelia Earhart continued to break records until 1937 when she attempted to fly around the world. Low on fuel, her plane disappeared over the Pacific Ocean. Mysteriously, no one knows exactly what happened. She may have ditched into the sea or crash-landed on a remote island. Whatever the truth, she will be remembered as a daring adventurer who broke down barriers for women and inspired a whole generation of female pilots to take to the skies.

→ Over the years, as Amelia Earhart's fame has grown, items such as her flying goggles have become very collectible and fetch high prices at auctions.

EXTRA

FEMALE HEROES OF FLIGHT

In the early days of flight, there were few women pilots. This made their achievements all the more incredible.

In 1912, Harriet Quimby became the first woman to fly across the English Channel from Dover, England, to Calais, France. The journey took 59 minutes.

Bessie Coleman was the first female African American pilot. She made a living by flying daring stunts at airshows during the 1920s.

In 1930, British-born Amy Johnson became the first woman to fly solo from England to Australia, just one year after gaining her pilot's license.

THE FIRST INTO SPACE

THE CHALLENGE	 To blast off in a tiny metal spacecraft and become the first person to leave Earth's atmosphere.
DANGERS Exploding on take-off; burning up or freezing to death; never returning to planet Earth	**WHO YURI GAGARIN** and a team of ground staff **WHERE** the Baikonur Cosmodrome, Kazakhstan, Asia **WHEN** 12 April 1961 **HOW** in his spacecraft Vostok 1, launched by a Vostok rocket **DISTANCE** 300 km (190 miles) high above the Earth **WHY** to prove that humans could conquer space as well as Earth
BACKGROUND	In the 1950s, the Soviet Union and the United States began competing with each other to develop rockets and send human beings into space. This became known as the Space Race.

Yuri Gagarin's space flight took 108 minutes from launch to landing. During that time he orbited, or circled, our planet once. He returned home a hero, making headline news both in the Soviet Union and around the world.

ТРИУМФ ЭРЫ СОЦИАЛИЗМА

Весь мир восхищен беспримерным подвигом советского народа

Пролетарии всех стран, соединяйтесь!

Коммунистическая партия Советского Союза

ЛЕНИНГРАДСКАЯ ПРАВДА

Пятница, 14 апреля 1961 года

ЦЕНА 2 КОП.

ЧЕСТЬ И СЛАВА!

Юрий Гагарин рассказывает...

Strapped in tightly with his helmet on, there was little for Gagarin to do but lie back in his seat and hope for a safe ride. The spacecraft was put under automatic control.

THE FIRST INTO SPACE

☞ Gagarin climbed into the spacecraft and waited for the countdown to start ...

↑ The Vostok rocket blasted off from the launch pad. One by one the rocket sections burned up and fell away until only the small spacecraft at the top was left to orbit the Earth.

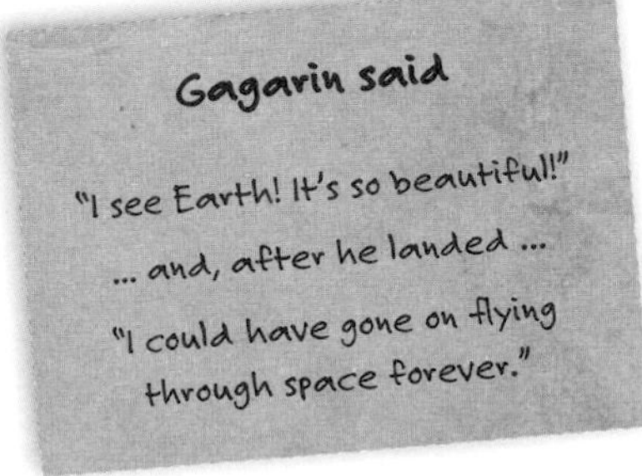

↑ In case of an emergency, Yuri Gagarin had enough space food to survive for ten days while ground control worked out how to bring him back to Earth.

Early in the morning of 12 April 1961, Soviet astronaut Yuri Gagarin was helped into his spacesuit and taken to the launch pad several miles away. Inside the spacecraft, he chatted calmly to ground control and waited for the hatch to be closed. If the launch went well, he would become the first human being to travel into space – but what were his chances of returning to Earth alive to tell the tale?

6.07 am The rocket engines rumble and Vostok 1 blasts off. Outside the spacecraft the noise is deafening, but inside it is strangely quiet and Gagarin feels only a slight shaking in his seat. He tells ground control, "Let's ride!"

6.17 am With a jolt, the spacecraft separates from the final section of the launch rocket. Gagarin is floating in space. Through the porthole, he can see the curve of our planet and the thin blue line that forms our atmosphere against the blackness of the universe. He reports that everything is well.

6.37 am He crosses the Atlantic Ocean and watches a spectacular sunset.

↑ This model of the Vostok spacecraft with planet Earth in the background gives a sense of what it would be like to float in space. Gagarin's cabin was inside the round capsule. This capsule was the only part of the spacecraft to come back to Earth.

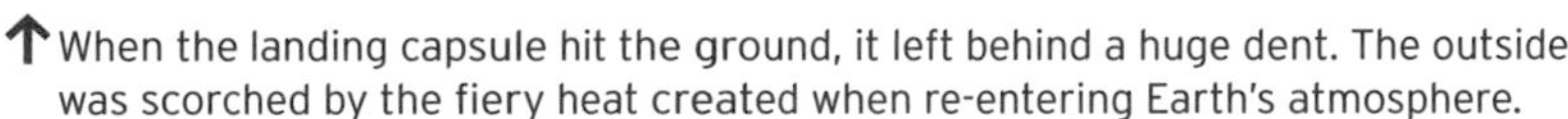
When the landing capsule hit the ground, it left behind a huge dent. The outside was scorched by the fiery heat created when re-entering Earth's atmosphere.

A Soviet postcard celebrates Yuri Gagarin's historic spaceflight. He also appeared on stamps and posters as a symbol of his country's amazing success.

7.10 am Passing over the Pacific Ocean, the sun rises. In just 33 minutes, Gagarin has witnessed both day and night.

7.25 am The spacecraft's engine fires over Africa, getting ready to re-enter Earth's atmosphere.

7.35 am The landing capsule separates but something goes wrong! The break from the spacecraft isn't clean. When the capsule finally shakes free, it hurtles toward Earth. Inside, Gagarin is thrown into a spin and nearly passes out.

7.55 am About 7 km (4 miles) from the ground, Gagarin is ejected from his seat as planned. His parachute opens and he glides back down safely to Earth. He has made history.

When news broke of Gagarin's achievement he became an global celebrity. He traveled the world promoting the Soviet Union while explaining that he was only a small part of a huge team. He came home to train other astronauts and to continue his previous job – flying jets. In the world's eyes, he was a hero and the Soviet Union had won the first round in the Space Race.

Yuri Gagarin died in a plane crash at the age of 34. This steel statue in Moscow, Russia, stands in the shape of a rocket. It is just one of many around the world to honor his memory.

SETTING FOOT ON THE MOON

How would it feel to walk on a giant dusty ball of rock in space?

The Saturn V rocket that launched the astronauts was the most powerful, heaviest and tallest rocket ever built.

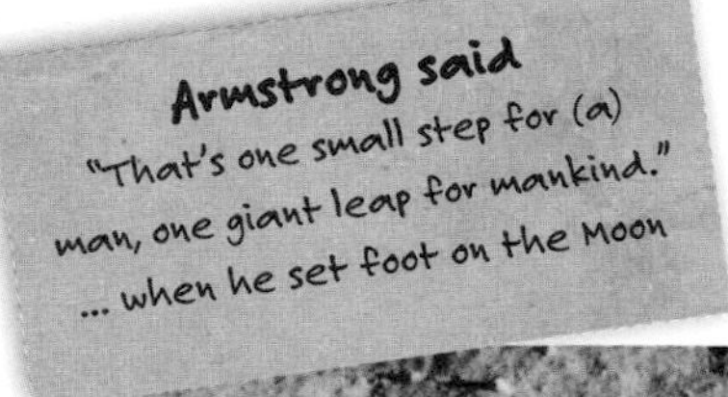

This footprint left on the Moon by the first astronauts is still there today, over 40 years later. This is because there is no wind or rain to blow or wash it away.

On 16 July 1969, with people all over the world glued to their TV sets, three men blasted off inside a metal rocket on a life-changing journey to the Moon. They had trained for and dreamed about this adventure for years – now it was real.

Take-off was smooth and 11 minutes later the men were in orbit. The rocket engines fired to line up their path and they began to cruise. Three days later, they were circling the giant rocky ball of the Moon, and the Earth looked like a small blue marble in the distance. Armstrong and Aldrin climbed into the lunar module, the part of the spacecraft that would land.

Neil Armstrong — Michael Collins — Edgar "Buzz" Aldrin

Three astronauts traveled to the Moon for the Apollo 11 mission but only two landed on its surface. Crew member Michael Collins remained in space.

THE RACE INTO SPACE
From the 1950s to the 1970s, the Soviet Union and the United States tried to outdo each other's achievements in space. In the mid-1970s, the Space Race ended and the two nations started to work together.

1957 October	1961 April	1962 February	1966 January
The Soviet Union launches Sputnik 1, the first satellite into space, and the race begins.	Soviet Yuri Gagarin makes history as the first person to orbit the Earth.	The United States catch up. They launch astronaut John Glenn into orbit.	Unmanned Soviet spacecraft Luna 9 is the first to land on the Moon.

↑ The lunar module was nicknamed "the Eagle." It touched down on a part of the Moon known as the Sea of Tranquillity.

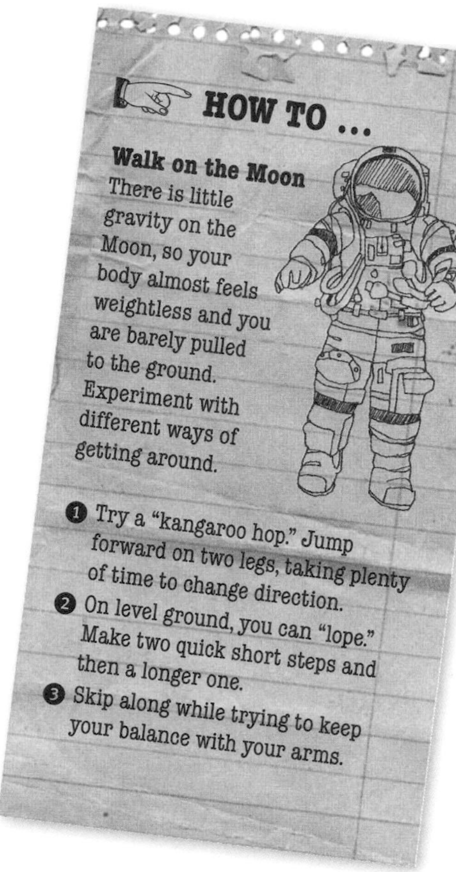

HOW TO ...

Walk on the Moon
There is little gravity on the Moon, so your body almost feels weightless and you are barely pulled to the ground. Experiment with different ways of getting around.

1. Try a "kangaroo hop." Jump forward on two legs, taking plenty of time to change direction.
2. On level ground, you can "lope." Make two quick short steps and then a longer one.
3. Skip along while trying to keep your balance with your arms.

Touchdown on the Moon's surface was hair-raising. First, an alarm sounded in the computer system, then Armstrong realized they were heading straight for a crater. With enough fuel left in the tank for just 30 seconds of power, he managed to steer the lunar module to a clearer patch and bring it down safely.

Six hours later, Armstrong and Aldrin climbed down the landing ladder. The whole world tuned in on their TV sets once more as the astronauts bounced about on the dusty ground and explored the cratered landscape. On 24 July 1969 they landed back on Earth safely, having made history. Over the next three years, the United States carried out five more Apollo missions and 12 people in total walked on the Moon.

↑ The cramped command module splashed down into the Pacific Ocean. It was the only part of the spacecraft to return to Earth.

1969 July	**1970 September**	**1972 December**	**1971 April**	**1973 May**	**1975 July**
The United States go further. Neil Armstrong and Buzz Aldrin walk on the Moon.	Unmanned craft Luna 16 brings back soil samples from the Moon for the Soviets.	The United States send Apollo 17 to the Moon as its final manned mission.	The Soviets launch their space station, Salyut 1, achieving another first.	The United States fight back and launch their first space station, Skylab.	US and Soviet astronauts shake hands in space and the Space Race ends.

TO THE OCEAN DEPTHS

THE CHALLENGE	 To dive record depths into the ocean and film a mysterious new world beneath the waves.
DANGERS Sharks and unknown creatures of the deep; running out of air under water	**WHO JACQUES-YVES COUSTEAU** and a crew of 25 scientists **WHERE** the Mediterranean Sea, the Red Sea and the Indian Ocean **WHEN** 1951 to 1955 **HOW** diving from his ship, the *Calypso*, with an underwater camera **DISTANCE** 22,200 km (13,800 miles) across different seas **WHY** to show the world the beauty and variety of underwater life
BACKGROUND	In the 1940s, Cousteau developed breathing equipment called the aqualung. This allowed him to move freely and spend longer periods of time under water than anyone else before.

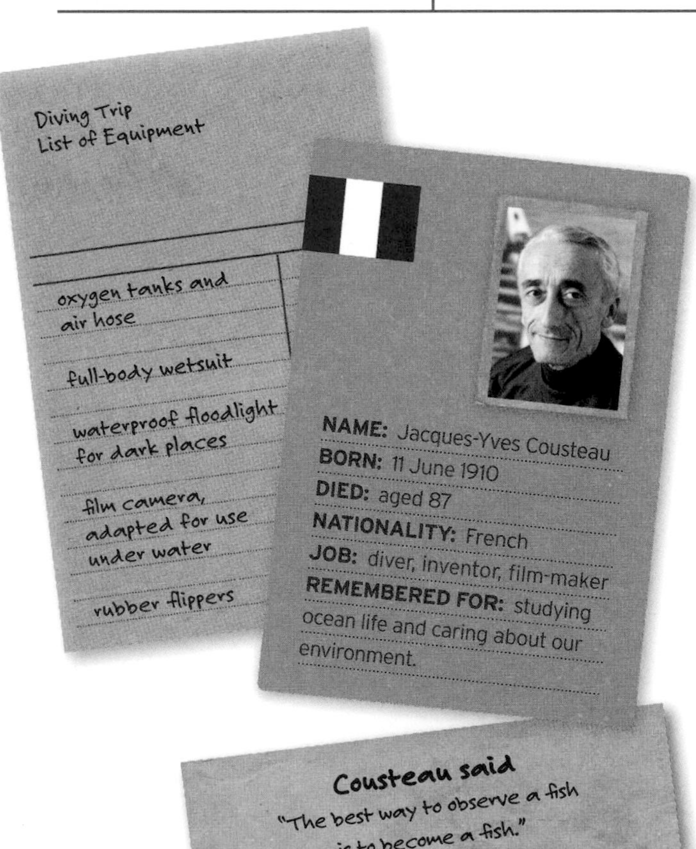

In 1951, Cousteau made a voyage to the Red Sea. Over the next four years, he sailed to oceans in other parts of the world, later writing a bestselling book and making a documentary film about these incredible experiences.

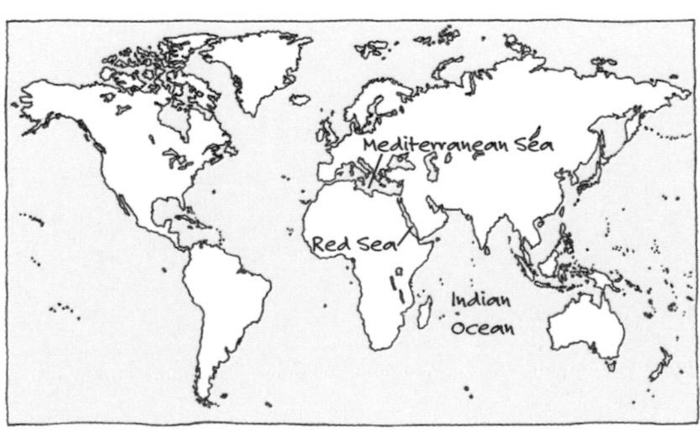

During his lifetime, Jacques-Yves Cousteau completed thousands of dives. Here he is filming life on a coral reef with a specially adapted underwater camera he developed. He named the camera "Calypso-Phot."

What mysteries were hiding for Cousteau and his divers under the sea?

↑ Cousteau made a documentary film called *The Silent World* about his experiences among the coral reefs. It was a huge success and, in 1957, won him an Academy Award.

In 1951, Jacques-Yves Cousteau set sail from the port of Toulon in southern France with a team of divers to explore the world's warm oceans. They sailed in a research ship, called the *Calypso*, kitted out with a laboratory for studying sea life and mapping the ocean bed. On these underwater adventures, Cousteau visited coral reefs swarming with rare tropical fish, swam with giant sea turtles and watched sharks in a feeding frenzy. He captured it all on camera in close-up and brought this previously secret world to the public for the first time.

The expeditions were dangerous. Cousteau and his crew dived deeper than anyone had done before, with a limited amount of air in their tanks. If they came back up to the surface too quickly, they would suffer from a sickness known as "the bends." Symptoms included joint pain, headaches and confusion – without treatment it could lead to death. They filmed ferocious sharks from inside a metal cage as the fish butted against the bars.

↓ Wearing his rubber wetsuit and scuba equipment, Cousteau prepares for a dive with two colleagues.

FEARS!

BE PREPARED

Could you ...

- **>> face a group of hungry sharks?**
- **>> explore dark caves and vents?**
- **>> dive down 75 m (256 ft)?**

The World War II cargo ship SS *Thistlegorm* lay undisturbed under the sea for about 12 years until Cousteau and his team discovered it.

During the trip, Cousteau discovered a long-lost shipwreck at the bottom of the Red Sea. From it, his divers raised a rusty motorcycle and the ship's bell. He also visited a remote sandy beach where he filmed baby turtles hatching and making their long, dangerous journey back to the water.

The expeditions were just a small part of Cousteau's life's work. As well as revealing the beauty of undersea life to us, he wanted us to protect it. He was one of the first people to warn against oil pollution in seas and the dangers of over-fishing. Thankfully, his message lives on through his family, who have continued his research and magical film-making adventures.

The research ship *Calypso* was customized to include an underwater viewing gallery. It also had special portholes so that divers could slip directly into the water through the bottom of the boat.

EXTRA

INCREDIBLE INVENTIONS

To make his undersea explorations more effective, Cousteau came up with many pioneering inventions.

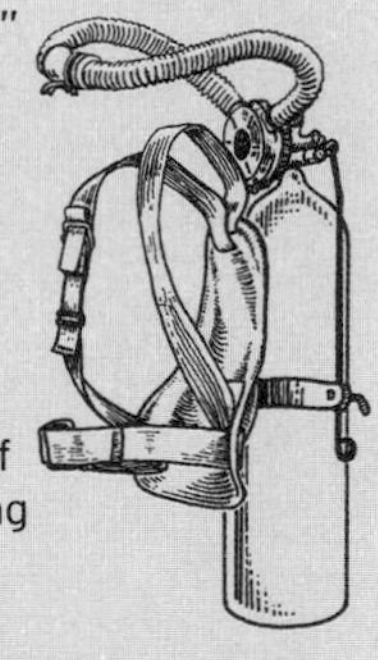

The "aqualung," which gave divers the freedom to breathe and move freely underwater, led to the development of the scuba-diving equipment we use today.

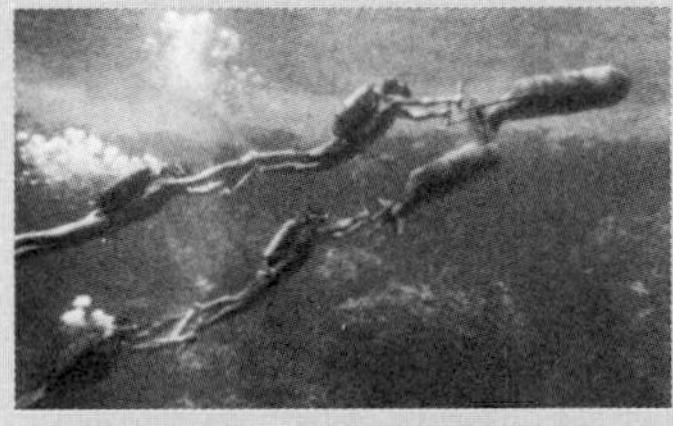

While making *The Silent World*, the divers used motorized scooters. They held onto the back and were propelled through the water.

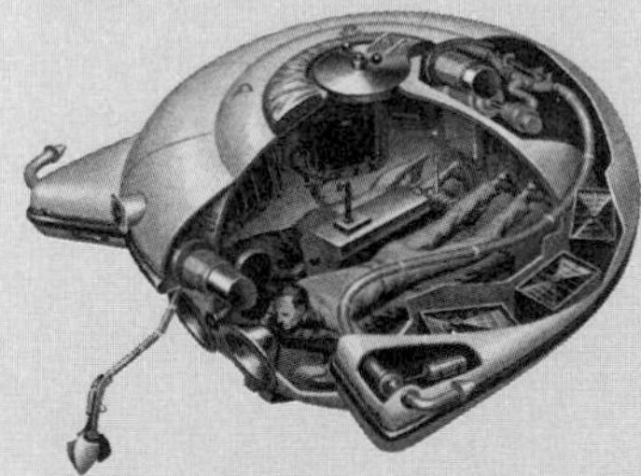

In 1959, Cousteau launched this diving saucer, a small submarine for scientific exploration. It moved like a squid, drawing in water from the sea, then shooting it out the back. He nicknamed it "Denise."

EXTREME CHALLENGES

THE CHALLENGE	 To journey to both the South and North Poles on a single grueling expedition, using only surface transport.
DANGERS Frostbite; your body going into shock from the cold; getting trapped on the ice	**WHO RANULPH FIENNES** and his explorer companions **WHERE** Antarctica and the Arctic **WHEN** September 1979 to August 1982 **HOW** on foot, by Ski-doo, by four-wheel drive and by boat **DISTANCE** 160,900 km (100,000 miles) **WHY** to push himself to the limit in a challenging environment
BACKGROUND	Fiennes was no stranger to tough challenges and adventures. He had previously served eight years in the British Army and been a member of the SAS, one of the elite British Special Forces.

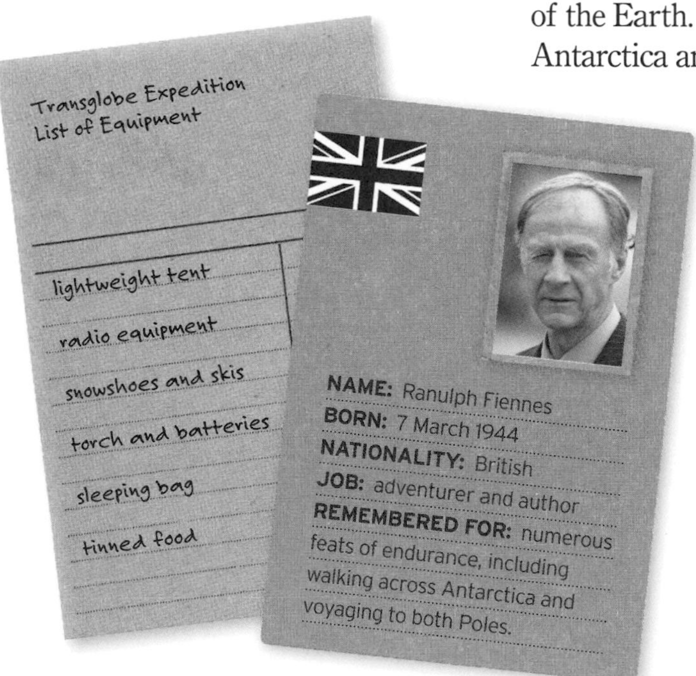

The epic expedition took Fiennes to the opposite ends of the Earth. He traveled first to the South Pole in Antarctica and then to the North Pole in the Arctic.

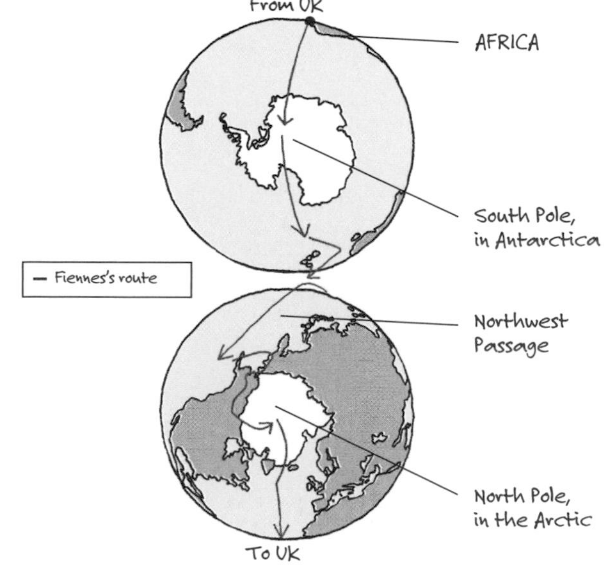

Fiennes adjusts his rucksack on a cliff in the far north of Canada on his way to the Arctic.

☞ Fiennes was about to battle the forces of nature. Who would win?

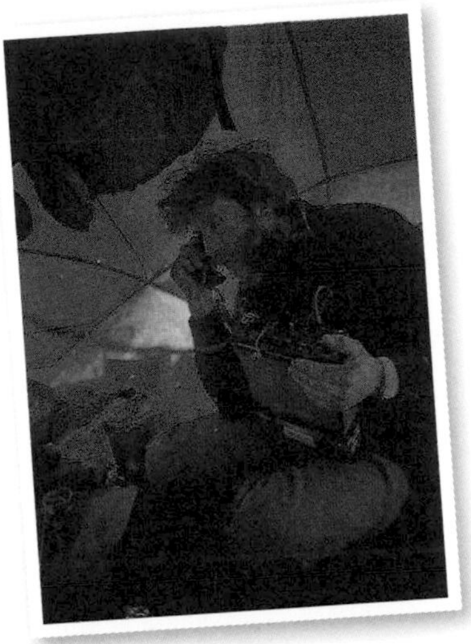

↑Sitting inside his lightweight tent in the freezing cold, Fiennes talks on the radio to the backup team at base to tell them about his progress.

HRH Prince Charles, expedition patron, said
"There will always, thank God, be people like the Transglobe Explorers ready to risk death in order to achieve something spectacular."

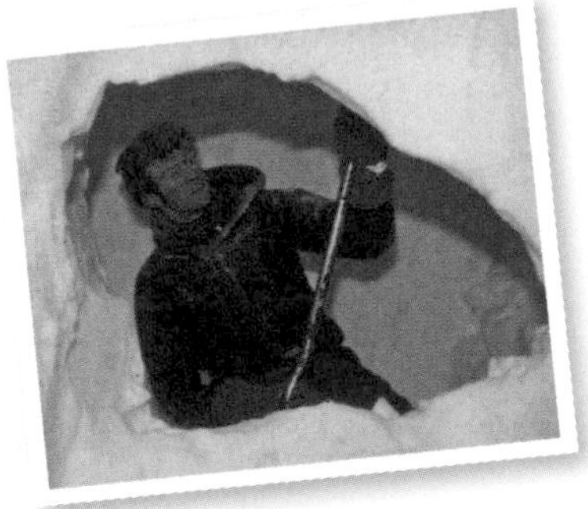

↑Fiennes digs a storage tunnel.
→Supplies were stored underground in storage tunnels to keep them safe and dry. Here, Charles Burton, the expedition "cook," looks for food for the explorers to eat.

It took seven years of planning and raising money before Ranulph Fiennes's dream, to travel from the UK to Antarctica and then up to the Arctic in one go, got off the ground. The Transglobe Expedition was going to be the first journey of its kind. The plan was for Ran, as he was known to friends, to travel using only surface transport – skis, sleds, Ski-doos, Land Rovers and boats. He would cross the harshest environments on our planet, including a burning hot desert, a vast, frozen continent and a deadly icy ocean.

September 1979 to December 1979 – The Sahara
Ran and his team of explorers (including his wife Ginny and Charles Burton), set off through Europe, then sail to North Africa. By the time they reach the Sahara, the largest hot desert in the world, the heat has kicked in and insects bite relentlessly. Getting up at 5 am each morning, the group climb into Land Rovers and drive. Winds whip up the sand and create violent storms. Ran thinks it's the easy part of the journey!

December 1979 to January 1980 – To Antarctica
Traveling on the *Benjamin Bowring*, a ship specially built for icy seas, Ran and the team arrive at the Antarctic coast. They spend several days unloading supplies and moving them to a safer place. The temperature here is as low as -50 °C (-58 °F).

DANGER!

WATCH OUT

Deadly threats ...

- **>> freezing cold winds**
- **>> raging blizzards**
- **>> terrible whiteouts**
- **>> treacherous ice ridges**

↑ Around the South Pole, ridges of ice break up the flat surface like a plowed field. Over many years, the wind has eroded the ice to create sharp peaks.

January 1980 to April 1981 – Crossing Antarctica
Ran and two other expedition members, Charles Burton and Oliver Shephard, make the Antarctic crossing. Despite wearing five under-layers of clothing, padded jackets and face masks, everyone is still frozen to the core. Traveling by Ski-doo, they can barely see as winds stir up the snow. The ice is not smooth so they bump along, worried about rolling off their vehicles and getting crushed.

As they head toward the South Pole, they cross sharp ridges of ice, known as sastrugi. These sastrugi fields stretch for miles and are treacherous. At times it becomes almost impossible to find paths for the Ski-doos to travel along safely. But finally, on 15 December 1980, they arrive at the South Pole Station.

Ran is keen to continue crossing the continent – there are still over 1,400 km (900 miles) to go! The team sets off across ice fields and glaciers, through ferocious winds. Descending to lower ground, they zigzag past deadly cracks in the ice, finally reaching the coast. They have crossed Antarctica in 67 days.

EXTRA

GETTING AROUND

Take a closer look at some of the vehicles Ranulph Fiennes used to complete his journey across the desert and polar lands.

Land Rover This four-wheel drive car was perfect for crossing the desert. If it got stuck in the sand, the explorers unloaded the car to lighten it before trying to move it.

Ski-doo With skis and tracks instead of wheels, these motorized vehicles are designed for traveling along flat stretches of ice. The team attached sleds to the back piled up with supplies.

Pulk When the ice became too bumpy for Ski-doos, Ran and his team switched to pulks. These canoe-like sleds could be loaded up, then pulled along by an explorer on skis.

Fiennes was about to battle the forces of nature. Who would win?

The *Benjamin Bowring* had a specially reinforced hull so that it could cut through the large blocks of ice floating around the coast of Antarctica and in the Arctic Ocean.

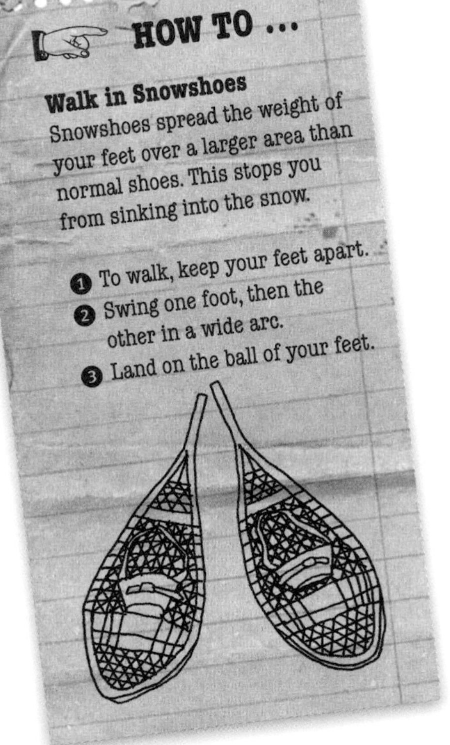

HOW TO ...

Walk in Snowshoes

Snowshoes spread the weight of your feet over a larger area than normal shoes. This stops you from sinking into the snow.

1. To walk, keep your feet apart.
2. Swing one foot, then the other in a wide arc.
3. Land on the ball of your feet.

May 1981 to September 1981 – The Northwest Passage
After sailing to the far north of the world, Ran and Burton, the only two expedition members on this leg of the journey, head upriver across Alaska and Canada. They then travel along the Northwest Passage, a 1,400 km (900 mile) sea route through the Arctic Ocean between icy islands. The passage lives up to its tricky reputation as they struggle through dense fog and get trapped in areas blocked by ice. Finally they find a stretch of open water and make it through.

September 1981 to August 1982 – Crossing the Arctic
Ran and Burton rest over the winter so they are fit for the final part of the journey – a punishing trek across the Arctic. They set off on Ski-doos but hit ice ridges so they switch to using pulks, which they pull along on foot. It is tough going.

Fiennes sailed this boat, the *Morgan Stanley*, through the Northwest Passage. Here he has just picked up a can of fuel to power the outboard motor.

A BORN ADVENTURER
During his life, Ranulph Fiennes has completed many feats of endurance and broken all kinds of records. Despite his increasing age, he shows no signs of stopping. Here are his incredible achievements so far.

1969
Leads a hovercraft expedition up the River Nile, the longest river in the world.

1979–82
Spends three years on the Transglobe Expedition, trekking to both the North and South Poles.

1992
Discovers the lost city of Ubar in Oman on the Arabian Peninsula.

1993
Becomes the first person to cross the Antarctic continent on foot.

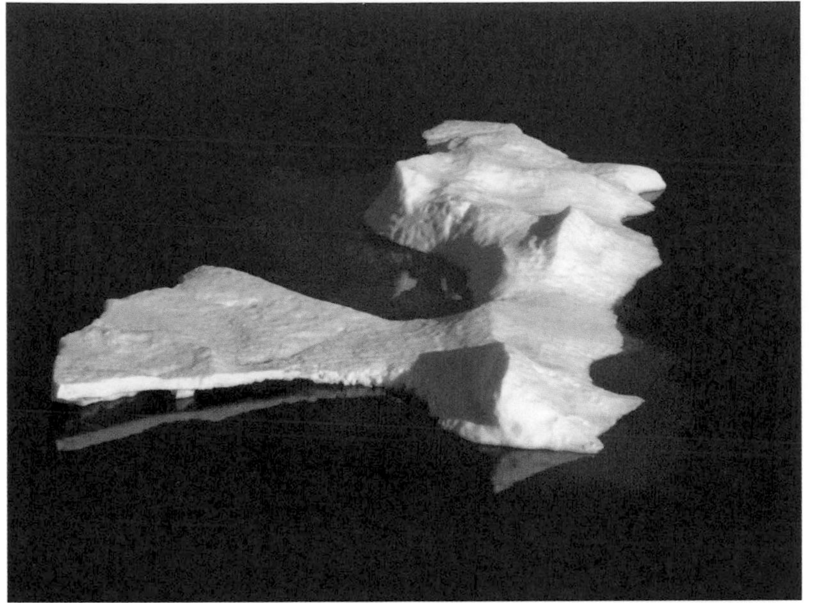

An iceberg drifts in the Arctic Ocean. For part of the journey home, the explorers floated along on a giant ice floe until the *Benjamin Bowring* could meet them.

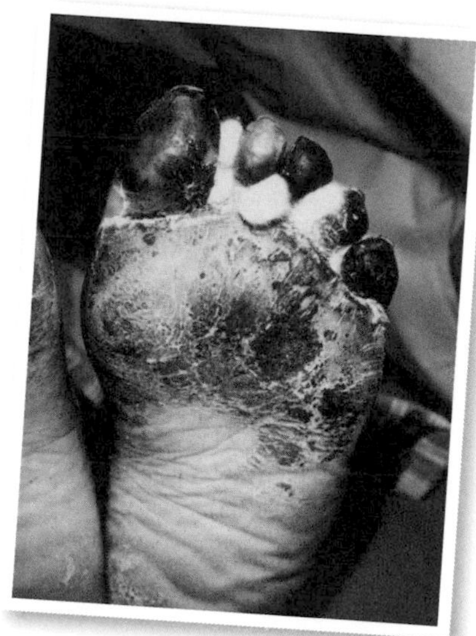

A case of severe frostbite. Sometimes with serious frostbite, the only treatment is to amputate the affected part of the body.

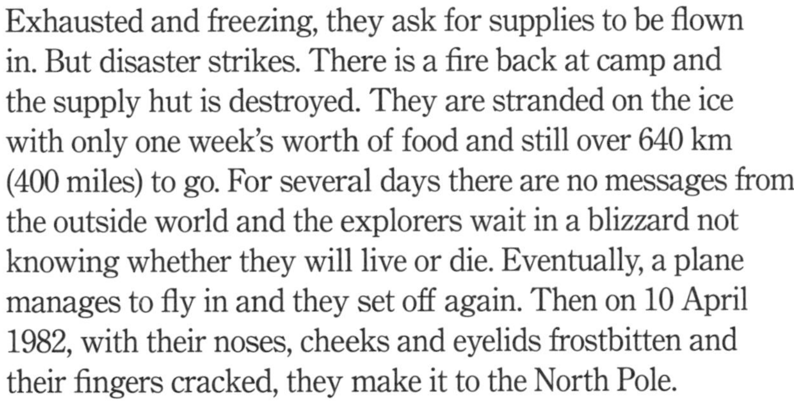

Exhausted and freezing, they ask for supplies to be flown in. But disaster strikes. There is a fire back at camp and the supply hut is destroyed. They are stranded on the ice with only one week's worth of food and still over 640 km (400 miles) to go. For several days there are no messages from the outside world and the explorers wait in a blizzard not knowing whether they will live or die. Eventually, a plane manages to fly in and they set off again. Then on 10 April 1982, with their noses, cheeks and eyelids frostbitten and their fingers cracked, they make it to the North Pole.

By August 1982, Fiennes and Burton are back in England. They have become the first people to travel from Pole to Pole on one expedition, and to have crossed the whole of the Northwest Passage from west to east in an open boat. Fiennes still takes on many extreme challenges. Perhaps that is why he is described as the world's greatest living explorer.

There was one extra-special member of the expedition – Bothie the dog, a Jack Russell terrier who belonged to Fiennes's wife, Virginia. Bothie became the first dog ever to visit both the North and South Poles!

2000	2003	2007	2008	2009	2012
Attempts to walk solo to the North Pole but fails. Back home, saws off the tops of his fingers due to frostbite.	Completes seven marathons in seven days on seven continents.	Despite a fear of heights, climbs the treacherous north face of the Eiger, a mountain in the Alps.	Takes part in mountain marathons, running up hills over two days with a rucksack.	Successfully climbs Mount Everest, the world's highest mountain at the age of 65.	Announces plans to lead a team on foot across Antarctica during the southern winter.

EXTREME EARTH

Our incredible planet is filled with natural wonders for us to explore. Discover some of the most extreme places on Earth.

WHERE	LAND
HIGHEST MOUNTAIN	Mount Everest in the Himalaya, Asia
HIGHEST VOLCANO	Ojos del Salado, in the Andes, South America
LONGEST MOUNTAIN RANGE	The Andes, running along the west coast of South America
LONGEST RIVER	The River Nile, which flows through northeastern Africa
LARGEST LAKE	The Caspian Sea in Asia, enclosed by five countries including Russia
HIGHEST WATERFALL	Angel Falls, in Venezuela, South America
WETTEST PLACE	Mawsynram in India where nearly 18 m (59 ft) of rain falls a year
DRIEST DESERT	The Atacama Desert in Chile, South America
HOTTEST DESERT	Death Valley in the United States, North America
COLDEST PLACE	Vostok Station, Antarctica, with a temperature of -89.2 °C (-128.5 °F)
SMALLEST CONTINENT	Australia, covering an area over 7 million sq. km (3 million sq. miles)
LARGEST CONTINENT	Asia, which is five times bigger than Australia

WHERE	OCEAN
LARGEST OCEAN	The Pacific Ocean, covering over one third of the Earth's surface
SMALLEST OCEAN	The Arctic Ocean, surrounding the North Pole
DEEPEST TRENCH	The Mariana Trench in the Pacific Ocean
SALTIEST SEA	The Red Sea in the Middle East, western Asia
LARGEST CORAL REEF	The Great Barrier Reef, off the coast of Australia, in the Pacific Ocean
TALLEST WAVE	The Gulf of Mexico, September 2004, with a height of 27 m (88 ft)

INDEX

akg-images 20br; Alamy: Everett Collection Historical 84l, © Chris Hellier 29ar, INTERFOTO 79ar, Mary Evans Picture Library 52br, © Marion Kaplan 68r, North Wind Picture Archives 25a, 39, 41al, Photos 12 86al, Pictorial Press Ltd 40br, © RIA Novosti 7r, 77, © Royal Geographical Society 5bcr, 91br, 93br; Art Archive: Gianni Dagli Orti/Science Academy Lisbon 19, Gianni Dagli Orti/Museo Correr Venice 35; Beinecke Rare Book and Manuscript Library, Yale University 23; Gertrude Bell Archive, Newcastle University: (340) 5bl, 66al, (K218) 65, (338) 66ar; Jim Fotheringham/Chris Bonington Picture Library 2; Bridgeman Art Library/Collection of the New York Historical Society 43; Cambridge University Library 52al; National Library of Australia, Canberra: Rex Nan Kivell Collection (NK3) 28ar, (an9184924) 29br, (an9308864) 29cr; Canterbury Museum, New Zealand 8l, 11a, 11b; Corbis: © Yann Arthus-Bertrand 29bl, 94l, Bettmann 73, 75ar, 86br, © Mukunda Bogati/ZUMA 60l, 94cl, Courtesy Richard Doyle 70br, © Rune Hellestad 88l, © Joanna Vestey 62al; Dreamstime: © Achim Baqué 93al, 94r, © Shariff Che'Lah 66cl, © Chenyun Fan 36br, © Frhojdysz 87al, © Legrandbleu 61, © Tyler Olson 91cr, © Sharon Yanai 91ar, © Zambezishark 70ar, 70cl, 94cr, © Jan Zoetekouw 49al; Eland Publishing 67br; Fototeca Storica Nazionale 7cl, 34l; Museo Navale di Pegli, Genoa 14r, 71c; Gernsheim Collection, Texas 5ac, 47; Getty Images: Thomas J. Abercrombie/National Geographic 87bl, David Meltzer/National Geographic 87br, Popperfoto 9, 10b, Time Life Pictures 7cr, 72r; Museum für Kunst und Gewerbe, Hamburg 5ar; Peabody Museum of Archaeology and Ethnology, Harvard University 44bl; Hull Daily Mail Publications 75br; Independence National Historical Park, Philadelphia (on loan from the City of Philadelphia) 42c, 42r; iStockphoto.com: Robyn Mackenzie 24al, Constance McGuire16r, Mlenny Photography 24bl; from M. Kingsley, Travels in West Africa, London, 1897 53al, 53cr; Kobal Collection: FILMAD/FSJYC 87cr, Turner Network Television 4r, 85; Museu de Marinha, Lisbon 4c, 18l, 20a; Museu Nacional de Arte Antiga, Lisbon 21ar; British Library, London 16al, 20bl, 28bl, 32al, 33a, 37br; British Museum, London 40al; National Maritime Museum, London 31; National Portrait Gallery, London 50r, 67cr; Natural History Museum, London 12bl, 13b, 52bl, 41; Courtesy George Lowe 55; Museo Naval, Madrid 25b; Public Library, Medford, Massachusetts 74al; Reinhold Messner Archive 62ar, 62bl, 63b; Missouri Historical Society, St Louis 45br; NASA 5al, 80al, 81, 82al, 82bl, 82br, 83al, 83br; Yale Center for British Art, New Haven 16bl; Newark Museum, New Jersey 17a; Germanisches Nationalmuseum, Nuremberg 21al; Joslyn Art Museum, Omaha, Nebraska 44a, 44br, 45al; Ashmolean Museum, Oxford 37bl; Bodleian Library, Oxford 36al; Pitt Rivers Museum, University of Oxford 7cr, 51, 68c, 69, 70al, 71b; Monastery of the Rabida, Palos, Spain 15; Parham Park Collection, West Sussex 32bl; Bibliothèque Nationale, Paris 37al; Pearson Scott Foresman 87ar; Athenaeum of Philadelphia, 76.16, Gift of Milton Hammer 45bl; Princeton University Library, New Jersey: Historic Maps Collection 24br, Rare Books Division 22r; George Palmer Putnam Collection, Courtesy of Purdue University Libraries, Karnes Archives & Special Collections 74bl, 75bl; Thijs Rommens 79br; Royal Collection, Her Majesty Queen Elizabeth II 32cl; Royal Geographical Society, London 13a, 48al, 48br, 49ar, 54c, 54r, 56al, 56ar, 56bl, 57ar, 57bl, 57cr, 57br, 58ar, 58bl, 59ar, 59bl, 59br, 66br; Science & Society Picture Library/Science Museum 53br, 78br; Science Photo Library: Seth Joel 78bl, Detlev van Ravenswaay 76l; Sir Ranulph Fiennes/Scott Polar Research Institute 89, 90al, 90bl, 90br, 92al, 92br, 93ar; Biblioteca Colombina, Seville 16cl; National Air and Space Museum, Smithsonian Institution: 75al, Eric Long 74br; from A. M. Stoddart, The Life of Isabella Bird, 1906 67ar; SuperStock: © age fotostock 67al, Norbert Wu/Science Faction 91al; Australian National Maritime Museum Collection, Sydney 32cr; National Palace Museum, Taipei 36cl; TopFoto/© RIA Novosti 78al, 79al; Topham Picturepoint 8r; U. S. Air Force 80ar; Library of Congress, Washington, D.C.: Geography and Map Division 5br, 41cr, Rare Books and Special Collections Division 38r, 41br; Museum of New Zealand, Te Papa Tongarewa, Wellington 30l; Alexander Turnbull Library, Wellington, New Zealand 26l, 27. All other artworks: Kavel Rafferty © Thames & Hudson

For my father, Max

On the cover *Front* 19th-century woodcut illustrations showing a ship and a man with a telescope. *Back* Dr. Wilson making sketches outside his tent. Photo Herbert Ponting © Popperfoto/Getty Images

Designed by Karen Wilks

First published in 2013 in hardcover in the United States of America by Thames & Hudson Inc., 500 Fifth Avenue, New York, New York 10110

thamesandhudsonusa.com

Library of Congress Catalog Card Number 2012947783

ISBN 978-0-500-65013-4

Printed and bound in China
through Asia Pacific Offset Ltd